PRAISE FOR
Remodel This!

"*Remodel This!* is as funny as it is useful. I have remodeled two homes in the past two years and if I had had this book I would have saved not only tons of money but also my SANITY."
— *Halle Berry* —

"Don't even THINK of remodeling your house until you read this book!"
— *Cheryl Ladd* —

"Toss the magazines, turn off the TV, tell your designer you'll call her back, and READ THIS BOOK! Robyn and Laura tell it like it is—from the hidden problems that lurk behind the walls to the emotional highs and lows of remodeling. All you have to do is look at the table of contents to see that this book will help you straighten out the mess you'll run into with your contractor, neighbors—even your spouse—before it has even begun! Get to know the nuts and bolts before you become a nut and want to bolt!"
— *Peri Gilpin* —

"Finally a step-by-step guide that helps you deal with all the craziness that comes with home renovation! I wish I had had this book last year when I was going through my own renovation hell . . . it would've saved me a lot of heartache—that's for sure!"
— *Eva Mendes* —

"*Remodel This!* is a must-read for any intelligent woman (and man if you're lucky) who's considering a remodel: it helps you ask the right questions and provides the answers in a fun-to-read, informative style. The experience of remodeling has really been captured in these pages, all while giving extensive advice on how to avoid or at least deal with the inevitable dramas that happen during the process."
— *Lisa Loeb* —

continued . . .

"My husband and I have just come through a year of remodeling hell. There is no more painful process other than childbirth. Any help should be gratefully inhaled. This book comes not a minute too soon in this world called remodeling. Nobody shows up. Everyone lies. So read this book, you'll really need it. It is a refreshing, fun aide and will make your life easier!"

— *Catherine Hicks* —

"This book clearly and realistically shows what a woman faces when she sets out to remodel her home. Unlike other publications out there on this subject, none do it from the woman's viewpoint quite like this. It tells you 'what to watch for' as you take your first steps in any remodel effort . . . and it injects a sense of humor into the subject as it walks you through examples of the pitfalls and the personalities you are likely to run into. Robyn and Laura's extensive legal background and knowledge of the subject are a godsend to everyone."

— *Jenny McCarthy* —

"Would that I had this book when I first bought my house—the grief and low-grade anxiety it would have dispelled! I can't wait to put its principles into practice when I remodel again."

— *Jennifer Beals* —

"At last—a roadmap to what to expect when remodeling that's informative and fun to read! As a contractor, one of my biggest challenges can be to educate a client on everything from budgets and schedules to delays and snafus, and our working relationship is bound to suffer unless she can start out her project with realistic expectations and accurate information. Now I have the perfect book to give to my clients to get us off on the right foot!"

— *Richard C. Nazarian* —

General Contractor and owner of the design-build firm
The Nickel Company in Los Angeles

"Ah, *Remodel This!* has arrived! Constant surprises? Upheavals? Mess, mess, mess??? How to organize, who to call, how to choose, how to stay sane and together through this process—it's all there and more, with the salsa added! Here is the book that I have been waiting to stock in my office for all friends and clients who decide to jump in headfirst. A real gem and the real dirt (literally) regarding this singularly frustrating but hopefully wondrous experience. If you read this first, it will be the latter!"

— LM *Pagano* —

Interior Designer, LM Pagano Design

"With wit and wisdom, Robyn and Laura have turned the daunting process of remodeling into a fun conversation between girlfriends. As a financial planner, I particularly appreciate their sage advice and helpful tips on what it takes to figure out a realistic budget."

— *Alice Finn* —

CEO of Ballentine, Finn and Company, Inc.,
named by Worth *and* Bloomberg Wealth Manager
as one of the top wealth advisers in the United States

"In *Remodel This!* Robyn and Laura humorously decode and decipher the 'what,' 'when,' and 'how' of one of the biggest challenges you can face in a lifetime—a home renovation. Peppered with amusing anecdotes and abundant information, these pages provide a roadmap for tackling the technical, legal, and interpersonal aspects of remodeling—and provide you with assurance that you are not alone any time you feel like pulling the plug or succumbing to feelings of inadequacy!"

— *Tina F. Kahn* —

Real Estate Lawyer, Partner,
Bloom, Hergott, Diemer, Rosenthal, and LaViolette, LLP

LAURA MEYER AND ROBYN ROTH

Remodel This!

A Woman's Guide to Planning and Surviving the Madness of a Home Renovation

A PERIGEE BOOK

A PERIGEE BOOK
Published by the Penguin Group
Penguin Group (USA) Inc.
375 Hudson Street, New York, New York 10014, USA
Penguin Group (Canada), 90 Eglinton Avenue East, Suite 700, Toronto, Ontario M4P 2Y3, Canada
(a division of Pearson Penguin Canada Inc.)
Penguin Books Ltd., 80 Strand, London WC2R 0RL, England
Penguin Group Ireland, 25 St. Stephen's Green, Dublin 2, Ireland (a division of Penguin Books Ltd.)
Penguin Group (Australia), 250 Camberwell Road, Camberwell, Victoria 3124, Australia
(a division of Pearson Australia Group Pty. Ltd.)
Penguin Books India Pvt. Ltd., 11 Community Centre, Panchsheel Park, New Delhi—110 017, India
Penguin Group (NZ), 67 Apollo Drive, Mairangi Bay, Auckland 1311, New Zealand
(a division of Pearson New Zealand Ltd.)
Penguin Books (South Africa) (Pty.) Ltd., 24 Sturdee Avenue, Rosebank, Johannesburg 2196, South Africa

Penguin Books Ltd., Registered Offices: 80 Strand, London WC2R 0RL, England

While the authors have made every effort to provide accurate telephone numbers and Internet addresses at the time of publication, neither the publisher nor the authors assume any responsibility for errors, or for changes that occur after publication. Further, the publisher does not have any control over and does not assume any responsibility for author or third-party websites or their content.

REMODEL THIS!

First edition: March 2007

Perigee trade paperback ISBN: 978-0-399-53315-0

An application to register this book for cataloging has been submitted to the Library of Congress.

PRINTED IN THE UNITED STATES OF AMERICA

10 9 8 7 6 5 4 3 2 1

PUBLISHER'S NOTE: This publication is designed to provide accurate and authoritative information in regard to the subject matter covered. It is sold with the understanding that the publisher is not engaged in rendering legal, accounting, or other professional services. If you require legal advice or other expert assistance, you should seek the services of a competent professional.

Most Perigee Books are available at special quantity discounts for bulk purchases for sales promotions, premiums, fund-raising, or educational use. Special books, or book excerpts, can also be created to fit specific needs. For details, write: Special Markets, The Berkley Publishing Group, 375 Hudson Street, New York, New York 10014.

To the loves of my life, my wonderful
husband, Neil Meyer, and my three amazing sons,
Kyle, Casey, and Thomas. In memory of
my beloved grandfather, Robert Singer.

Laura Meyer

To my mother and father, Sharlene and Mike Roth,
for always reading everything I ever wrote.
And in memory of Lawrence H. Greaves,
my law partner, mentor, and friend.

Robyn Roth

Acknowledgments

WE WOULD LIKE to acknowledge the many people who helped make this book possible. We start with our agents, Dan Strone and Melissa Flashman of Trident Media Group, who believed in our book from the start. We would also like to thank everyone at Perigee, including our marvelous team of editors: Michelle Howry, who was our book's original champion at Perigee; Christel Winkler, who gave us her extremely helpful input and enthusiastic guidance as we wrote; and Meg Leder, who took us through the finish line with her exceptional edits. We are grateful, too, for the efforts of our lawyers, Neil Meyer and Erin McPherson, who gave invaluable counsel along the way.

We also wish to thank some very special people who assisted us in navigating the world of publishing: Stephen Breimer, Judith Karfiol, Maureen Kedes, Margo Lane, and Maureen Peyrot.

A special thank-you goes to Richard Nazarian of the Nickel Company, general contractor extraordinaire, whose insights into the contractor's perspective on remodeling proved invaluable. We also thank talented interior designer, Etienne DeCludt, for his expertise and assistance.

We appreciate the enthusiasm and support of all of our clients, colleagues, and friends, as well as their war stories, many of which provided inspiration for parts of this book. Thank you, Catherine Glaser, Cheryl Kolbor, Marsha Metz, Jolie Schifino, Ellen Waggoner, and Stephanie Yates.

Finally, we are grateful to our families for their continuous patience, love, and encouragement while we were writing this book. Robyn wishes to acknowledge her parents, Sharlene and Mike Roth, and grandparents, Max and Grace Gottlieb, for their unwavering love and support; Jeffrey Roth and Teri Roth, who know the agony and the ecstasy of remodeling as well as anyone, and Amanda Roth and Brandon Roth. Laura wishes to acknowledge her loving and supportive husband, Neil Meyer, and three sons, Kyle, Casey, and Thomas, who have a love of books and are "excited to see Mommy's name on a book at the bookstore." Laura also wishes to acknowledge her mother, Doris Glick Rubin, who is always there to support her through anything and everything; her father, Al Glick; and Andrew Glick, Dan Rubin, Evelyn Meyer, and Carolyn Meyer.

Contents

Introduction

YOU'RE THINKING ABOUT remodeling. We know what's on your mind. We also know what you may be in for if you're not careful.

The fantasy: You find your perfect home right away. It's on the perfect street and in the perfect neighborhood. It's in move-in condition, but with all the money you saved on the purchase price, you decide to make a few changes anyway, just to make it your own. Your contractor is attentive, organized, and reliable— oh, and he's really nice to look at, too! He even finishes on time and under budget. In fact, by the time you're done remodeling, he's practically family. This wasn't painful at all. What were your friends complaining about?

The reality: *Where is your perfect home?* By the time you have picked up this book, no doubt you have been asking yourself this very question. Perhaps you recently purchased a home that is either too small, not in good shape, or not done to your taste. Or it could be that you have lived in your home for a while and are ready to make some much-needed changes. You're excited to start your project, but you're also a little nervous about the whole thing because you've heard that remodeling can be quite an ordeal.

Consider the story of one woman who did not know what she was doing, and soon found that her home renovation was out of control:

Susan got the name of a contractor from a friend of a friend. They met and she really liked him. It all seemed so perfect—Gus promised to start the work right away (a kitchen and master bathroom remodel) and to finish by November 15—in time for her to enjoy her home with her family during the holiday season. Gus seemed to understand exactly what she wanted to accomplish, and certainly told her what she wanted to hear.

In a rush to start her remodel, Susan hired Gus without seeing any of his prior work or checking his references. She even signed his form contract without really reading it or reviewing it with anyone more knowledgeable. That didn't matter to Susan at the time, and when demolition began days later, as promised, she was thrilled!

But that feeling didn't last long. As soon as Gus's workers opened up the walls, they found a termite buffet. Those little bugs were feasting in her kitchen before Susan could! More bad news followed . . . in the form of cloth-covered electrical wiring (a fire hazard from the 1920s and 30s), corroded galvanized plumbing pipes that needed to be replaced, and work done by the previous owner that was not to code and needed to be corrected.

Suddenly, the project was several months behind schedule, and Susan was staring at a stack of unexpected bills. Eyeballing her incredibly shrinking bank balance, she panicked. How could her beautiful home betray her like this?

And where was Gus, anyway? He was so attentive before she wrote him that first check. But then, just when things were getting complicated, he seemed to disappear. He stopped answering his cell phone and often didn't return Susan's calls—this from the same man who called her three times a day when they first met. Then he conveniently forgot to tell her about yet more delays and extra costs until it was too late for her to make appropriate plans. Gus had seemed so professional at the beginning.

In response to this shabby treatment, Susan started acting nervous and needy around Gus. It wasn't her style, and she resented him for making her behave this way. She knew her project was not the only one, but she still thought she was special. His broken promises disappointed her.

Trust turned into betrayal. Adoration became seething rage. Susan's faith in Gus was shattered. She hated him.

Pretty soon, Susan learned about problems with Gus from his prior clients and realized that the contract she had hastily signed was missing some very important protections. And she could forget about her project being completed before the holidays. At this point, she would be lucky if the work would be done by spring!

Now Susan was not only mad at Gus but was also angry with herself; she should have known better. After all, her friends and family had tried to warn her with their own nightmare stories. But she didn't listen. She didn't think it could happen to her! Only after it was too late did she realize that, not only hadn't she paid attention to advice and warnings but she also had no idea what she was doing. She didn't have a clue about how this whole construction thing actually worked.

WHY WE WROTE THIS BOOK

Susan's story is all too typical of a remodel gone bad. While home renovation has become a national craze, most women have little or no understanding about how the remodeling process works or what to look for in a contractor, even though they are often the ones making many, if not most or all, of the decisions. And even if she thinks she knows what she's doing, a woman never really knows what she's getting herself into until she gets started. We know . . . it happened to us!

We both have extensive backgrounds in the world of real estate and have been close friends and colleagues for years. As lawyers, between the two of us, we have represented some of the most prominent people in Hollywood in their construction projects, negotiating touchy contracts, advising on complicated financial and legal issues, resolving sticky situations and holding clients' hands through some very trying times. We have also seen or represented many of these same clients through divorces, sometimes precipitated by remodels gone bad and usually involving lots of real estate.

So you would think, with all of this professional expertise, we'd be more than prepared for the renovations of our own homes. But instead, we were caught off guard by the obsession, frustration,

He Could Be a She

Throughout this book, we assume your general contractor will be a man. That's because, even in this day and age, the vast majority still are. And because the construction business in general is male dominated, we think it's important to address the male–female dynamic. You'll probably be dealing with a lot of that. Of course, there are some female contractors out there. If you hire one, rest assured that our advice in this book applies equally to her, although the interpersonal dynamic may be a little different: either she could be your new best friend or the relationship could get pretty catty!

anger, excitement, and confusion that gripped us in the thick of our own projects. It became clear to us that even professionals cannot escape the emotional ups and downs of a home renovation. We also saw that, as women, we had issues while renovating that only our girlfriends could understand.

We searched for a book that could guide us through the remodeling experience. Yet every book we found was dry and textbook-like and didn't address many of the problems we faced. So like all good girlfriends, we turned to each other. As we commiserated, we realized that every woman dreams of "Mr. Right Home." We learned that (contrary to conventional wisdom) you really can change him—that is, when *he* is your house. We became addicted to home shows and design magazines—our women's porn. (We indulged, usually in private and never in front of our men or the kids.) Avid shoppers already, we shopped till we dropped—not for shoes but for knobs and fixtures, the must-have home accessories. Each of us talked incessantly about the new man in our life—our general contractor.

And because one of us is married with three children and the other is single, we debated whether it's better to live with "the man who knew too much" (the too involved mate) or the clueless man (the uninvolved mate) or whether doing it solo is easiest of all. We became each other's therapists, offering advice on coping and making it through.

At first, these fun observations and analogies were our secret survival strategies. They quickly evolved into invaluable professional tools for counseling clients and friends differently from the way we had before. When we saw how appreciative our female friends and clients were, not just of the professional advice but also of the personal tips, we realized that it was time to share our insights with a broader audience.

PART 1

Getting Things Started and on the Right Track

1

Beauty and the Beast:
AN INTRODUCTION
TO REMODELING

A WOMAN CAN spend years yearning for "House Charming" to show up, with exactly the right number of bedrooms, the ideal floor plan, and done just to her taste—all at a price that she could afford. But a woman who is serious about a piece of real estate quickly learns that all of these qualities usually do not come in one package.

It can take a lot of work to get a relationship with a home right. And some homes take more work than others—the whole thing may need to be changed or just a part of it. Either way, the basic rules of remodeling—from planning the job to choosing the right contractor—are the same.

Although the prospect of a home renovation can be daunting and intimidating, remodeling has significant benefits:

- **Getting what you want**. When you remodel your home, chances are you'll love what you end up with. Sure, it can be a lot less trouble to move into a home that is move-in ready, but the truth is, you'll be paying a premium for someone else's work and you probably won't like everything about it.

Avoiding the Guilt!

*M*any people want to buy a move-in-ready home because they think the hassle and expense of remodeling will be too much for them. Down the road, however, they end up seeing a lot of things about the place they don't like and want to change. Most people feel guilty ripping out something that is in perfectly good condition and that they paid a lot of money for. On the other hand, with a fixer, there's nothing but joy when demolishing something that's already outdated, a mess, or doesn't work.

- **Getting what you can afford.** You may not be able to find an affordable, move-in-ready home in the ideal neighborhood. Or the affordable move-in-ready home you do find involves a commute too far from work, friends, family, and civilization as you know it! Buying a place that needs some or a lot of work may be the best way to get what you want in the area you want to live in. If you are first looking for a home and are the type that can see the potential in a beast, then buying a fixer might even be a fairy tale come true. Just because the sellers live like pigs, the grass is dead, and the bathrooms are outdated with crumbling tile is no reason necessarily to reject a home. You can easily address these cosmetic turn-offs. Other factors that aren't so easily fixed (like location, location, location) may be much more important.

- **Keeping what you love.** There may be things about the home you live in that you just can't replicate somewhere else. It could be some special feature or unique quality about the home or property—like that magnificent view—that made you fall in love with it in the first place.

You just need to make some tweaks so that you can be happy with it again.

- **Staying where you feel comfortable.** If you already have a favorite dry cleaner and know your local pharmacist and if your morning walks with your next-door neighbor are the highlight of your day, then why move when remodeling will accomplish all your goals?

- **Making an investment.** A remodel done the right way can increase the value of your home. We talk more about this in Chapter 6.

Diamond
in the Rough

Not every woman has the ability to spot potential in a home, in much the same way as a woman might reject a man on the first date because of his ugly haircut and dorky shoes, completely missing the fact that he picked up the check, held the door open for her, made her laugh, and spoke well of his family. Soon, some other woman snatches up this great guy. You could make the same tragic mistake with a home and let some other woman nab your dream house! You could be repelled by defects that can easily be changed and be blind to the good points that not every piece of property can or will have.

THE REMODELING ROAD MAP

Whether you are renovating a single-family residence, condo, or co-op; whether you are remodeling on a small or grand scale; or whether you are doing it alone or with a spouse or partner or children in tow, you'll need essential information:

In Part I, we show you how to get off on the right foot with everything and everyone in your life. You'll learn how to plan effectively for your remodel, from design to budget. We also clue you in on what to expect on the personal front and how to keep your life—and your moods—under control!

Part II gives you the inside track on how to hire the right people for the job. You'll learn about hiring contractors, designers, architects, and other people you may require for the job. We give you a primer on your construction contract as well as tips for how to deal with your cast of construction characters when problems arise.

In Part III, we tell you about the actual construction process, from what you'll need to take care of before and during construction to helping you understand how it all works and what happens when. Plus we give you shopping tips for becoming a savvy construction consumer.

Part IV takes you across the finish line, with tips for getting your contractor to finish up those last few things and helpful hints for settling in or moving in once the work is all done.

THE BENEFITS OF OBSESSING OVER YOUR REMODEL:
Doing Your Research

Some women have known all their lives exactly what their dream house would look like, down to the style of knobs on the cabinets and the color of the front door. Other women start out with a vague notion that they need to make a change but aren't sure what it is that they want to do. Yet even the woman who thinks she knows what she wants may not have as much information as she should. She may be married to the idea of her home looking a certain way only to realize after it's too late that she would have gone in a different direction if she'd had a little more knowledge. As you dream and obsess about your remodel, you may wonder if you'll make the right choices. One of the best things you can do in the beginning stages is to search for things that inspire you. Here are some good places to start.

Surfing the Net

Any time of the day or night, you can type a few key words about any remodeling topic into your favorite search engine and find websites and articles galore on every conceivable kind of product or service from all over the world. Are you curious about where to get different types of stone? Want to find out about different types of appliances or fixtures? Looking for unique antique hardware or more affordable reproductions? You can find virtually anything you want and can check out configuration, finishes, brands, styles, and prices of everything at just the touch of a button. It's a good idea to print out pictures of and information about items that appeal to you.

Magazines and TV Shows

You've probably noticed that home magazines line every newsstand and that there are more shows on television now than ever before devoted to home renovation and home design. If you're like many women, you may already be obsessed with reading or watching them. Why read a novel when you can read about the hottest new developments in kitchen gadgets instead? Rip out and save the pages of anything that inspires you.

Seeing It in 3-D

Sure, that under-the-counter wine cooler looks great in its Internet photo and profile, but there's nothing like meeting in person. A good way to get your creative juices flowing is to visit design showrooms and see other people's remodels. If you have friends who have remodeled, then—no doubt—you'll be checking out what they did. If you're intrigued by your neighbor's remodel, don't be shy about asking if you can take a peek inside. If you love the color of your friend's living room, write down the brand, color name, and type of finish. Find out where your cousin bought

---

HGTV Is Women's Porn

*I*t can be her biggest turn-on and she can't get enough! Unfortunately, although it's fun to watch, many women are fooled by skin-tight schedules, tidy plots, tiny budgets, and airbrushed photos. . . . These TV shows often peddle just the sexy fantasies. Use your research—and this book—to see the truth behind the glamour so that you don't have unrealistic expectations.

---

her tile. Write down the name of the woman who painted the glaze on her dining room walls. And, once you start interviewing contractors or designers, you should ask to see other homes they've worked on or designed. It's a good idea to take a camera with you so that you can photograph things you like. Digital photos are today's form of instant photographic gratification, and they can be especially useful because they are easily e-mailed to designers and contractors who need to know in which direction you want to take your remodel.

GET IT TOGETHER:
Assembling Your Remodeling Portfolio

Before you know it, you've got a purse full of scraps of paper with phone numbers, clippings all over your house, printouts from your Web searches piled on your desk, and paint samples everywhere. Do yourself a favor—get organized! There are a number of things you can do to make your life a lot easier, things that will also enable your contractor, architect, designer, or anyone else who is helping you get a handle on your vision. So, instead of writing things down on loose pieces of paper and on the backs of business cards, carry a pad with you so you can have your notes all in one place. Get some file folders and create a filing system. You can organize your clippings, business cards, and samples room by room or you can organize them by trade (for example, painters) or by category (for example, appliances). The more organized you are, the more together you'll feel.

2

I Want This:

PLANNING TIPS
FOR THE MOST COMMON
AND COVETED HOME RENOVATIONS

*F*OR ANY REMODELING project, you will want to focus on both form and substance—what you want something to look like, on the one hand, and what you need and what is practical for your lifestyle, on the other. The woman who focuses on form *over* substance can get herself into trouble: When she bought that pedestal sink she fell in love with for her bathroom, she completely lost sight of the storage space she so desperately needed, which could have been provided by a vanity. And after she'd finally gotten those retro black-and-white checkerboard kitchen floors she'd always wanted, she started to hate them as soon as she realized that they showed every speck of dirt her kids, their friends, and assorted pets tracked in the door.

It is easy for a woman to get carried away and fall in love with something because it looks great or to become obsessed with some cool appliance that she just has to find a place for. And we know that's part of the fun! But it's only part of the equation. Whether you will be making design decisions yourself or looking to a professional for help, this chapter will help you focus on some of the important practical considerations for some of the most popular remodeling projects.

THE KITCHEN IS IN

The kitchen has always been an important room. For many, it is the hub of the house. For families, it is often the place where everyone congregates and where kids do their homework or art projects. But even for people living alone and for people who can barely boil an egg, there is no question about it—everyone wants a great kitchen.

If you are remodeling a larger space and have a big budget, you may be after your dream kitchen, complete with all the bells and whistles: high-end appliances, a fabulous island for everyone to sit around, a walk-in pantry, a separate breakfast area that doubles as a family-room, and maybe even a built-in desk to use as a workspace. Butler's pantries, which traditionally separated the kitchen and the dining room, are also now coveted features in high-end kitchens and have become extensions of the kitchen wherever they may be placed. If your budget or space is tight, then your goals are probably less grandiose. With a tight budget, you

The Remodeler's Wish List

Before you start your remodel, it is a good idea to make a room-by-room list of things you both want and need and to rate those items as either essential or desirable. This list can be helpful in a number of ways. It will help you focus on the details of your project; it will help any professional you are working with to get a sense of what you want to accomplish; and if you are on a budget and need to trim costs when your estimates come in, it will help you figure out what you can and can't live without.

Research Your Materials

$\mathcal{I}$n selecting your materials (flooring, countertops, etc.) you need to be informed. For example, you may love the look of limestone countertops in the kitchen but hate how easily limestone stains. If you are the kind of person who likes that lived-in look, then you may not be bothered by this. But if stains will drive you crazy, then this material is probably not right for you. Ask a lot of questions and know what you are getting yourself into as you make your choices. Think about things like water, heat, and stain resistance and how slippery certain surfaces are (like marble bathroom floors). Think about your lifestyle and who is living in your home. Also, if you really love the look of something but find out it's not the most sensible choice, check out practical alternatives that you will like. For example, if you like the look of marble countertops in a kitchen but want the stain and heat resistance that granite offers, you may be able to find granite that looks just like marble.

may be looking to reface cabinets rather than replacing them, which is a great—and less expensive—way to achieve a whole new look. And when you don't have much room to work with, you're probably focused on making the best use of the space you do have. Either way, here are some planning tips.

Don't You Hate It When . . . ?

A good starting point for planning your new kitchen is to think about what you don't like about your current one. For example, you feel like you never have enough light (lighting issues are very important in a kitchen and should not be overlooked) or you hate that there's no place to store the knives and forks near your breakfast nook. Maybe you hate when people are in your way when you entertain. You know that no matter how hard you try to get guests to sit in another room while you're cooking in the kitchen, you just can't keep them out. If only there were a place for them to comfortably hang out so they won't make you crazy!

What Works?

There may be things about your old kitchen that have worked well for you. For example, you may have no problem with the current location of the main appliances—your stovetop/oven, dishwasher, and refrigerator. If that's the case, then keep the configuration the way it is, because it can be very expensive to move things like water and gas lines.

Are You an Eat-in or Take-out Kind of Gal?

If you and your family like to eat in the kitchen, then you'll want to make sure you have space for seating. Seating can be around an island, along a countertop, and/or in a separate eating nook. If you have a small space but this an important feature, consult with your contractor or a designer about creative solutions. You may have little ones that you're desperate to keep out of your fancy dining room. Simply gaining two or three seats could make all the difference.

Efficiency and Working Side by Side

In a small kitchen, it may be hard to avoid feeling cramped the minute more than one person walks into the room. You want to make good use of the space you have. So imagine the different tasks you will be doing and where it would be best to place everything from appliances to cabinetry. For a larger kitchen, it's a good idea to think about designing the space around separate work stations: a prep area, an area for washing dishes, a cooking area, and so on. Kitchen utensils should be stored in close proximity to where you will be working. And you may want to consider having two sinks or getting a microwave that doubles as another oven. This way, a number of people can work comfortably together and not feel like they're on top of each other.

For Large Families and the
Gourmet Chefs of the World

If you have a large family and/or frequently entertain and cook for a lot of people, storage will be key as will lots of usable counter space. A walk-in pantry ranks high on many homeowners' wish lists, as does an island work area. If you don't have the space for a walk-in pantry, consider how you can maximize your cabinet space so that you can have as much storage as possible. And if you cook a lot, you will also want to have easy access to your pots and pans by the stove.

One Thing Leads to Another

*I*n remodeling, some choices you make can require more work than you think. For example, in choosing a restaurant-style range, you will need to have a restaurant-style ventilation system. The installation of one could add a lot to your budget or may not be possible at all for structural reasons or because certain local regulations forbid it. Also, some flooring requires subflooring, whereas other flooring does not. As soon as you have figured out which appliances you might want or what materials you think you'll use, talk to your contractor about any special accommodations they may require.

Cleanup

The dishwasher, sink, and counter space make for a good cleanup station. Consider where you will be storing your clean dishes, glasses, and cutlery. You may want to have storage space for those things in close proximity to your dishwasher. And speaking of dishwashers, if you have a large kitchen and feed a lot of people on a regular basis, consider getting two of them. Cleanup becomes a beautiful thing.

Selecting Appliances

Every kitchen has certain basic appliances—a refrigerator, oven, and stove. Most kitchens also have dishwashers and garbage disposals. Built-in microwaves are common, too. But what about all the other great appliances out there? Food warmers, refrigerator and freezer drawers, and built-in cappuccino makers, to name just a few. Before you start your remodel, you should make a list of all the appliances you would like to have and then get the spec sheets that list the dimensions of the model you like. You can cut or reconfigure cabinetry to fit your appliances, but you can't shrink a dishwasher.

Flooring

The kitchen is one of the places in the home where the floors get the dirtiest and need to be cleaned regularly. Whether you choose tile, linoleum (which has made somewhat of a comeback with new and improved choices), a composite floor (which can be made to look like hardwood), hardwood, stone (both of the latter are favorites in upscale kitchens), or another material, consider maintenance issues, how slippery the material is (tile sometimes comes in a nonskid finish), and—if you spend a lot of time standing in your kitchen—how the material is on your back. Many people don't know this, but hardwood has a lot of give to it and is much easier on the back than a harder surface like stone or tile. The downside to hardwood is it can warp if it gets wet.

Outlets and Hookups

For your major appliances, your contractor should know exactly what hookups you'll need. But you may want to install outlets in places that no one is focusing on. For example, if your kitchen has an island and you will be using that space to place warming trays when you have a party, then you'll need to have a spot to plug them in. And don't forget hookups you may want for your TV and computer.

BUILDING AND BATHROOM BASICS:
From Spa Bathrooms to Elegant Powder Rooms and Everything in Between

Bathrooms are usually the smallest rooms in the house. But make no mistake about it—it is still easy to spend a fortune on the bathroom of your dreams. And if you're like most women, you can probably justify this expense to yourself because you likely spend more than your fair share of time there!

A bathroom can truly become your home spa and oasis. There are so many luxurious ways to go: from large showers with waterfall showerheads to spa tubs featuring specialized jets (for massaging you head to toe), and built-in television and audio systems. All you need is a phone and a glass of wine and you'll be able to lock the door behind you for hours.

When remodeling a bathroom, aside from addressing things like ventilation and the hot-water supply, probably the most important consideration is who will use the bathroom.

The Master Bath: Special Considerations

- **Your own space**. Most upscale master bathrooms are designed to have two sinks, a toilet in its own compartment, and a separate tub and shower. Another nice feature in a master bathroom is a separate vanity area. If you have the room, separating the space into different areas is especially helpful if you're sharing your bathroom.

- **Are you a bath or shower person?** If bubble baths or long hot showers are your way of relaxing, then do your homework and know what's available. If you are in the market for a spa tub, then go to the showroom and hop into a bunch until you find one with the arm rests, leg rests, and jets in just the right places. Do you love your showers? A steam shower with a built-in bench seat may be just the thing for you.

- **Room for all your stuff**. Another important feature in a master bathroom is adequate storage and countertop space. If you are like most women, you've got a lot of stuff, and you want to keep your makeup, hair products, curling irons, and lotions out of sight!

- **Lighting**. And speaking of makeup, bathroom lighting is key. There's nothing worse than not being able to see what you're doing in the bathroom or starting the day off thinking you look awful because the lighting in your bathroom makes you look green. You'll want brighter light when you're getting ready to go out, but for relaxing in the tub or shower, consider installing dimmer switches.

Children's Bathrooms: Special Considerations

- **Is it safe?** Most bathrooms are designed for adult use. For toddlers and small children, the average bathroom is not particularly user friendly and can even be dangerous. Recognizing and addressing these issues will give you peace of mind and will help you design a bathroom that is a safer and more enjoyable environment for your child. For example, it's not easy for little ones to navigate adult-size toilets and sinks. You can install child-size counterparts that are smaller and lower but are compatible with standard plumbing so that they can be easily replaced with full-size fixtures when your children get older. Hot water also poses a danger. Consider a faucet with safety stops that has adjustable settings and restricts how far the handle can be pushed toward hot. There are also companies that are exclusively in the business of baby and child proofing. If you have a baby or young child, we would strongly recommend consulting with one of these companies (see Resources).

- **Looking ahead**. Kids' rooms and bathrooms are a lot of fun to design, but you'll want to think ahead or you may regret some of your decisions. For example, that cute tile with the hand-painted ducks may be great for your baby, but it will cost you a fortune to rip out and replace a few years down the road when your grade-schooler thinks it's "so uncool." So when choosing things like tile, consider something that will take your kids through the years. Have fun with accessories that are easy and inexpensive to change.

The Powder Room

If you have or are building a powder room (also known as a half bath because it does not include a tub or shower), you will not need to deal with a lot of the same things you worry about for a full bathroom. Beauty comes in all sizes—not much space is needed for a powder room, and any space, no matter how small, can look great. Focus on stylish design elements, accessories, and lighting.

BEYOND KITCHENS AND BATHROOMS:
Important Considerations for Remodeling Other Rooms

We have already walked you through some of the special considerations for remodeling kitchens and bathrooms. But there are a few other general considerations that apply to all rooms:

Reconfiguring Rooms by Adding or Removing Walls

Take a look at the space you have and ask yourself if it is being used in the best way possible. For example, you may be happy with the size of the master bedroom but may feel that the closet space is inadequate to house your wardrobe. Ask yourself if you would be happier with a smaller master bedroom that has more closet space. Or you may have a huge dining room that never gets used and would rather take some of that space to enlarge the kitchen.

Getting Wired

Whether it's the bedrooms, the family room, or that extra room that could be used as a guest bedroom, home office, media room, play room, or home gym, one of the most important things to consider is the location of electrical outlets and wiring for things like phones, sound, high-speed Internet access, and satellite and cable. Wiring often involves opening up the walls. Even if you were not planning on remodeling certain rooms now, if you think that updating your wiring is something you may do in the future, it may be more economical to do the work now while your contractor has the tradesmen lined up for other work—tradesmen who will need to be involved with the wiring work itself or with things like patching up and painting the walls after they have been opened up.

BUSTING OUT:
Building Additions

You might be adding on to your home because it has become too small for your family and you need an extra bedroom or bathroom or larger kitchen. Or maybe you're working from home a lot and need a designated home office. On the other hand, you could be adding more space just because you can. After all, how nice would it be to have a media room, home gym, guest suite, or wine cellar? Whatever your reasons for adding on, there are certain things you should know about building additions.

One of the most important aspects of adding on is to make sure the addition looks as if it had always been part of your home. (You have no doubt seen bad additions that look as if they were slapped on from another house—you may even be correcting one as part of your remodel!) Here are some things to consider and talk about with your contractor, architect, or designer.

Proportions Are Everything

There are a few key design elements that go into tying an addition to the rest of the home: The roof style and roof slope should match the slope of the roof on the existing part of the home (even if they are on different planes) and the roofing materials should be the same. Similarly, the window styles and sizes should be the same. An exception to this would be decorative windows that are meant to stand out such as leaded-glass windows. But even with these, it is important to match the style of the window trim. Also, in the interior, consider wall height. If most of the home has rooms with nine-foot ceilings, the addition will tie in better if you maintain the ceiling height for rooms that are on the same floor. There are, of course, exceptions, such as a great room or master bedroom that is designed with a cathedral ceiling.

It's All in the Details

If you've ever had a pair of jeans hemmed, you know that they just don't look the same as when you first bought them, unless the tailor matches the exterior stitching that appears everywhere else on the jeans. The color of thread and the type of stitching are designer details that add to the garment's character. Likewise, when adding on to your home, if you want the addition to look as if it were always there, you'll need to make sure the details in the addition match the details in the original home. Examples of things to match are window trim, doors, hardware, and the style of exterior railings. Even matching little things like the style and color of rain gutters that run along the exterior of the home can make a big difference.

To Mix, to Match, or to Start Anew?

Sometimes it's impossible to find readily available materials that will match what's already in or on your house. Don't fret. Rather than having to start anew, you may be able to get something custom made. So rather than replacing the whole roof because matching tiles are not available for the roof of an addition, you might be able to find a company that can duplicate what you've already got. Doors and moldings are just a few of the other things that can be custom made if necessary. Will this save you money? Maybe but not necessarily . . . you will always need to compare the cost of these alternatives.

CRAZY FOR CLOSETS

Sometimes, it just takes a little creativity to make the smallest room in the house satisfy a woman's desire for luxury. Other times, what is typically the smallest room in the house morphs into something that's the size of a bowling alley!

Gone are the days of the humble closet. The fifty-square-foot walk-in closet, once considered a luxury, is now standard in new construction of large homes, and, beyond that, super-size closets are all the rage. These huge closets aren't just for clothes and shoes, either—women also want flat screen TVs, sophisticated sound systems and phones, and even a separate place to sit and relax. And you can forget about cheap construction. Beautiful materials—like mahogany and maple—and elegant hardware are popular. It's much like the days when women had luxurious dressing rooms, but with today's high-tech spin!

Most women do not have the room in their home for so huge a private sanctuary. But you don't have to be Paris Hilton to have a great closet. Sometimes, even a few added features will make a relatively modest closet so much better. There are many closet companies out there that will help you make the best use of the space you have. They can outfit closets with jewelry drawers (which do not take up much room), shoe chambers (closets within closets just for your shoes!), and other creative features that are great for organizing all your stuff.

One last thing . . . consider getting a safe for your closet. It's a good idea to have a place to store some extra cash, important papers, and your bling.

THE IMPORTANCE OF GOOD LIGHTING

Any actress or model knows that lighting can show off her beauty when it's right, but can be her worst enemy when it's all wrong! And any good designer will tell you that good lighting is critical to the look of your home. Many people try to save money on their remodel by keeping the old lighting, such as outdated fixtures that don't go with the new look. But remember, you've spent a lot of money to make your place look great. Consider spending a little more to light it well.

TAKING IT OUTSIDE

Even a small outdoor space that's well designed can make your home feel so much bigger and can add that perfect spot for entertaining or a haven to escape on a Sunday afternoon with a magazine. Remodeling a large outdoor space can actually become an important—and costly—part of your remodel. Outdoor fireplaces, decks, gazebos, pools, hot tubs, and outdoor kitchens are big-ticket items, not to mention landscaping.

One of the biggest decisions to make when remodeling a large outdoor space is balancing hardscape (like stone and brick) with landscape (like grass and other natural ground surfaces). While it is nice to have a big expanse of lawn for kids to play on, if you will be doing a lot of entertaining, keep in mind that hardscape is much easier to walk on—especially for women wearing stiletto heels!

3

Therapy, Anyone?
REMODELING, YOUR RELATIONSHIPS, AND KEEPING A BALANCE

*I*T DOESN'T MATTER whether you are married, single, or divorced, working or not—remodeling is a time-consuming, nerve-racking, stressful endeavor that is bound to affect you and your personal life in one way or another. While you are in the beginning stages of planning your remodel, it's a good idea to start thinking about how you'll make it through—either together with your spouse or solo. And don't forget about the kids, if you have any. The upheaval will affect them, too. Even your relationships with the rest of your family, your friends, and your job may suffer. In this chapter, we give you some tips for keeping it together before things get out of hand!

REMODELING AND YOUR SPOUSE/PARTNER:
Staying Together While the Walls Are Coming Apart

From finances to design decisions, remodeling can be very hard on a marriage or relationship. Fights over money and disagreements over taste can really take their toll. If she is not careful, a woman might walk into divorce court before she and her husband ever set foot in their newly remodeled home! Let's take a look at different scenarios and how best to deal with potential problems.

Who's in Control?

Who controls the wallet? Who decorates the house? If he's happy to dole out the bucks while you design the home of your dreams or if you happen to be the lucky one who makes most of the financial and home decor decisions, then you're in good shape. But if the two of you are not on the same page about either money or design, then it's time to sit down and set some ground rules *before* work begins. Before you start, think what type of man you're dealing with.

The Man Who Knew Too Much

Simply put, he's too involved. What do we mean by this exactly? After all, this home is both of yours—you should be in this together, right? In theory, that makes sense; but in reality, most women are fiercely opinionated about how they want their homes to look. It's just one of those things that's hard to compromise on. The too-involved spouse is in your face every step of the way—he wants this remodel as much as you do. He has very particular tastes and cares about every little detail. He probably loves shopping for furniture, too. (Damn!) He wants to be involved from beginning to end. The good news is that, because he has such a vested interest in the end result, he's more likely to help you with everything from contractor problems to shopping for appliances. The bad news? It's pretty obvious—this could spell trouble in paradise if the two of you have divergent tastes—say, he wants modern and you want traditional or he wants a dark and masculine feel while you want light and airy. For the couple who fights about everything from paint color to the cost of bathroom tile, just know that if you can make it through your remodel, you can make it through anything! Also know that compromising on everything may not be the answer because you both could end up not liking anything. Talk about the things that are most important to each of you. In the end, one of you may care about certain rooms or features more than others. Consider each designing a room of your own.

The Middle-of-the-Road Man

He's not going to give you free reign, but it's possible to keep him satisfied! Sometimes, it just takes throwing him a bone—like committing to a game room in the basement, surround sound in the den, or *not* to paint the dining room lavender. This is his home, after all, and a reflection of his masculinity! Doesn't sound like too much to ask, does it?

The All-Too-Practical Guy

Is he a pain in the butt or the voice of reason? It's easy for a woman to forgo practicality in favor of something that looks great—like those dark wood floors you find so striking—that he quickly points out will show every footprint. "Wouldn't something else be a little less maintenance?" he asks. Okay, so you admit to yourself that he may be right, but it does take a bit of the fun out of it, and you're determined to have those dark wood floors anyway.

The Man Who Is Missing in Action

At first, it may seem like the man with a hands-off approach is the easiest type to deal with. "Anything you want, sweetie" or "Don't worry, I trust you" would be music to many women's ears. And, if he's footing the bill with his hard-earned dollars, he may think he's contributing enough. But, in the end, remodeling

Remodeling and Romance

*Y*ou're feeling grouchy because a few days have gone by and the workers didn't show up and he's sick of your constant whining about the contractor. Take some stress out of remodeling and put some romance back into your relationship—make a pact that at least one night a week you won't talk about the house and do something fun together instead!

is a stress-laden affair filled with many decisions and, often, unwelcome surprises and problems. You may end up resenting him big time if you're sweating it out alone while he goes off to work blissfully ignorant. If you find that you are overwhelmed and need him to pitch in, reel him in and let him know how he can best help you. While he may be clueless when it comes to interior decor, there's bound to be something that's up his alley.

Talking About Costs

If tempers have flared before over your shopping habits or over how much he spent on a car, then you may very well have differences over this one, too. Think about it: This is likely to be one of the biggest shopping sprees of your life. Trying to get on the same page before you start remodeling is not just about keeping the peace but is also about keeping costs down. Designers (who usually charge by the hour) have made a lot of money mediating couples' design differences. (In fact, there are entire television shows devoted to this topic.) And it can cost even more if the contractor has to change something midstream.

Keeping Him in the Loop

It goes without saying that, when planning your remodel, you and your partner should be in agreement about the budget. But, as we stress throughout this book, what you spend often ends up being far more than you had ever imagined it would be. There are many reasons for this. Even if your man is relatively uninvolved with the design angle of things, it is a good idea to have him come to any meeting at which changes to the plans are going to be discussed. These changes could involve fixing an unanticipated problem or adding something to the plans. Whatever the case may be, changes usually involve spending more money. You don't want him to go ballistic when he sees the bills, second-guessing you all the way, even though he has no idea what's been going on because he hasn't paid attention.

REMODELING AND THE KIDS:
"Mommy, I'm Talking to You!"

Everyone in the family will be affected by the disruption and chaos of remodeling, including the kids. Even if you just bought the home you are remodeling and can stay in your old home until the work is over, if your kids are old enough to realize what's going on, they may be affected by the anticipation of moving and may feel ignored as you become immersed in your renovation. And you, having taken on the responsibility of dealing with a remodel, are sure to have moments of feeling overwhelmed juggling kids, remodeling, and any other commitments you have in your life.

Doing Something So Everyone's a Little Less Cranky

So what can you do to make the kids feel a little less whiny about all the time that Mommy has been spending dealing with this project? Consider that your kids may be excited about being a part of it—choosing the color for their rooms or new bedding may make them feel better about the whole thing. And do yourself a favor by trying not to have little kids around when you're meeting with your contractor or other members of your remodeling team. (If the kids are home all day, try to get someone to watch them.) It will be a lot more pleasant for everyone, and safer for the kids, since the job site can be a safety hazard.

Safety First!

If you are living in your home as you remodel, the younger your kids are, the more difficult it will be. You'll be concerned about dangerous conditions such as debris, tools, nails, and other sharp objects lying around. Doors may be left opened as the workers come in and out and you or someone else will have to keep an extra careful eye on any little ones. Make sure you talk to your contractor about trying to keep the place as safe as possible as you live there through this mess. Your contractor will also need to secure dangerous areas, such as a hole dug for a pool. If there are special instructions that relate to the safety of your children, it's a good idea to put that in writing in your contract.

REMODELING AND THE SINGLE WOMAN:
The Adventure of Going Solo

If you are single, it is perfectly understandable to feel nervous about undertaking a home renovation on your own. Remodeling is a daunting prospect for any woman, and the idea of doing it alone can make you feel even more nervous.

However, know that you're certainly not the only one. In your parents' day, you might have been the only one on your block to be "remodeling single," but anyone who has been reading the newspaper or watching her neighborhood lately probably knows that times have changed. As a matter of fact, the 2000 census recorded for the first time that single adults outnumber couples with children as the most common type of household in the United States. And after married couples, single women are the largest segment of home buyers in the United States. You are part of a full-fledged phenomenon and a major demographic. So, as a single woman, what things should you keep in mind as you remodel?

There Are Advantages

We don't want to gloss over the unique concerns confronted by the solo remodeler. But let's not forget that there are definite advantages to not having to contend with the opinions, attitudes, involvement, and interference of a partner. Sure, you won't have someone else to lend moral support or help foot the bill. On the other hand, you won't have to deal with the typical spats that couples get into about design and money. So think of your glass as being more than half full!

One of the great things about being single is that you get to play house any way you like. You get to design your rooms to please just you. No one is going to try to talk you into making some ugly sports memorabilia collection the center of attention in your den, like your friend's football-maniac husband did when she remodeled. That same friend (who, by the way, must also share her closet with her husband and hide the shopping bags from him when she returns from her favorite department store) can't get her man to buy—or buy into—the style of kitchen she loves. But no one is going to second-guess your taste or spending habits when you design *your* kitchen. The ultimate decisions are all yours!

> ## Getting in Touch with Your Masculine Side
>
> Chick flicks play just as well as action movies on big-screen plasma TVs with surround sound. Don't let the guys have all the fun when you can get wired, too!

The Challenges

If you've ever walked by a commercial construction site, you've probably heard at least a few hoots and catcalls shouted at some hot woman walking by. Yes, men can be pigs, so you may be a little nervous about the construction site coming to you. But don't worry—most of the guys working on your site will be respectful and hardworking; they are often family men who would no more hassle you than they would let some hound dog bother their wives or daughters. Still, as in any male-dominated profession, it's possible that you'll run into some jerk who comes on too strong. And he might think you're fair game because you aren't wearing a wedding ring or coming to the site with a partner.

It's one thing to get hit on when you are in a public place, surrounded by people. It's quite a bit more disconcerting to have it happen in your own home. That's why you want to make sure you are comfortable with the crew who shows up on your doorstep. Still, no matter how careful you are and how well your contractor knows his team, problems occasionally crop up:

Meg, busy remodeling the house she bought after her divorce, didn't notice that Rex, the window subcontractor, was unusually attentive; he even called to set up an appointment for a Sunday to take measurements for the third time. It seemed odd that he'd have to do this three times, but Meg just thought that Rex was conscientious and wanted to do the job right. She liked that. But when he arrived, it soon became clear that Rex was more interested in Meg's measurements than those of the windows. The inappropriate personal questions made his intentions perfectly clear. Even the usual "I have a boyfriend" line didn't work on the apparently shameless Rex. An uncomfortable Meg showed him the door quickly and called her contractor, Harley, right away. Harley had a wife and two daughters, so he was particularly sympathetic. He told her that Rex was harmless—just a lonely guy who had just separated from his wife of many years. Even though Meg had a hard time getting over how Rex had used false pretenses to be alone with her, taking up her valuable time, and even scaring her a bit, she reluctantly agreed at Harley's urging to give Rex another chance. (Rex was, after all, Harley's best window guy.) But when Rex kept calling her for dates even after Harley told him to back off, Harley hired a replacement. Harley was much more careful after this incident about who he hired to work on jobs for his single-women clients.

If you encounter a personal problem with any member of your contractor's crew, make sure you address it with your contractor right away. If the problem happens to be with your contractor himself, there are a few things you can do. First, try to steer any personal conversations in the direction of the business of your remodel and hope he gets the hint. If he's persistent, you may feel too uncomfortable with your working relationship. Just make sure that you check your contract's termination clause first before you fire him.

REMODELING AND YOUR FRIENDS AND FAMILY:
Everyone's a Busybody

There are only so many hours in the day, and you soon may find that leisure time you previously enjoyed spending with family and friends is being filled by remodeling minutia. True friends and loving family should understand, especially those who have been through it. But people who haven't experienced the chaos, stress, and obsession of a home renovation for themselves might start resenting that you have disappeared off the face of the planet. And you are probably missing their company, too. So, as time permits, try to spend time with the ones you love. After all, you still want them to be in your life for the housewarming party!

Should You Involve Your Loved Ones?

One way you can have your remodel and spend time with your friends, too, is to include them when possible—especially if they have been through it before or are going through it at the same time. Sometimes there is nothing more fun or therapeutic than hanging out with your girlfriends, commiserating about the trials and tribulations of remodeling, and walking the construction site that your home has become. And let's face it, just like when you introduce your friends and family to a new man in your life, you might welcome the feedback and approval, too!

There is definitely a downside, though, to sharing your vision with your loved ones. Sure, sometimes you can get some great ideas. But some people cross the line and tell you what they *don't* like or what they *don't* think you should do when all you wanted to do is share this big thing in your life with them. This can put a damper in your relationship.

Lisa was close to her mother, Barbara, but their tastes could not be more different. Lisa didn't like her mother's big hair and ostentatious jewelry, whereas Barbara constantly got on her daughter's case about her plain Jane look. It was no surprise, then, that Lisa hated her mother's fancy home, which looked to her like a gaudy palace. It was also no surprise that Barbara did not particularly approve of the laid-back open floor plan, muted colors, and simple furnishings that figured so prominently in Lisa's remodel. Lisa was close to tears almost every time her mother came to visit the job site. After all the years of arguments, why couldn't her mother mellow out? She really wanted to share this with her mother, and she couldn't understand why it was so painful to hear what her mother had to say while it was so easy to accept tips and advice from her friends. The truth for Lisa was this: Barbara could offer *nothing but criticism, even when she didn't mean to. So Lisa stopped including her mother and instead turned to her friends, whose advice was much more constructive, even when critical. The good news is that after it was all over, Lisa and Barbara made up, and Lisa even uses the too-fancy-for-her-taste crystal glasses Barbara gave her when Barbara comes over for Sunday brunch.*

REMODELING AND YOUR JOB:
Fitting It All In

You've heard it from all your friends—remodeling isn't just an all-consuming obsession—it's a full-time job. That's a problem if you already have a full-time job. And you'd better keep the job that comes with a paycheck if you want money to pay for your remodel.

The key to keeping your day job during your remodel is to be very organized about your schedule and to be honest with yourself about what you can and cannot do at a particular time on a given day at work. It also means making sure that everyone you hire—but particularly your contractor—understands and agrees to work around your availability. Fortunately, most contractors start work early in the morning (often by 7 a.m.), before most people have to be in an office. You also want to make sure your team is sensitive to whether you can take calls at work and when. If you do have to take some time off during work hours, and if you are answerable to someone, make sure you give that person as much advance notice as possible. If you tell your

You and Your One-Track Mind

"Can't you talk about anything but paint colors?" If no one is saying this to your face, they are probably thinking it if all you can talk about is your remodel. So if you ask, "Do you want to talk about something else?" and everyone shouts "Yes!" then you'll know it's time to develop other interests . . . or keep quiet until you do!

boss that you are remodeling, and if your boss has been through one, too, you should get a lot more understanding.

Your remodeling project can also be a perfect topic of conversation at work, as long as you play it the right way. If you have colleagues at work who have been through it before, you'll probably want to commiserate but, like any personal matter, be careful about sharing too much information in a professional setting. No one at work needs to know exactly how much money you are spending or that you and your husband haven't had sex since the last Super Bowl because at the moment the remodel has (temporarily, one hopes) sapped every last sexual impulse you and he once had!

PRESERVING YOUR SANITY:
Don't Forget About You!

As work is about to start on your project, spend a few minutes reflecting on what it takes to keep you sane. Don't let yourself fall apart while your home is being put back together. You will feel bitchy enough as things inevitably go wrong during your remodel. But to add insult to injury, if your nails or hair are not done or you miss your favorite kick-boxing class, there is no telling what might happen! As a matter of fact, we would even recommend some additional pampering . . . which, by the way, is always good for a woman's soul. While massages and shopping sprees are always favorites, you may find that this is not the time to indulge in retail therapy or other costly pastimes. Besides, simple pleasures are often the best. There is great comfort to be had in coffee and lunch dates with friends, walks around the neighborhood (especially if you want to check out another remodel down the street), regular bubble baths, and a good night's sleep. Find something that makes you feel good. You'll need it!

4

A Simple Nip/Tuck or Extreme Makeover?

GETTING A HANDLE ON THE SIZE, SCOPE, AND BUDGET OF YOUR RENOVATION

O H, **WHAT YOU** could do with an unlimited budget! Inspiration is everywhere, staring you in the face, and you know how much better those tired old rooms could look. But now it's time to get down to business and plan out a realistic budget. You'll also have to figure out how to foot the bill. In this chapter, we'll show you how to get some idea of the size and cost of your remodel as you begin to plan. We'll also tell you about some options for paying for it.

TOO RICH OR TOO THIN:
The Dangers of Pushing Your Financial Limits

As a starting point for planning your budget, you should take a hard look at your finances and your lifestyle to make sure you don't take on too much. If your budget is tight, don't panic—you may not be able to do everything you want, but you can work with it so long as you do a lot of advance planning.

Marriage and Money

As we recommend in Chapter 3, if you are remodeling with a spouse or significant other, you should both feel comfortable with your remodeling budget. Remodeling can lead to the demise of a relationship, with fights over money being a big reason. Make sure you and your partner see eye to eye on this issue.

Part of figuring out how much money you can afford to spend often includes consulting with your accountant or any other professional or person you trust to guide you in your financial affairs. You can also talk with a lender who will tell you how much money you qualify to borrow. You may find that you qualify for a loan that lets you borrow more than you originally thought you could. But don't be lulled into spending the most you can afford because there is a difference between what you *can* spend and what you *should* spend. Don't take on too much debt or spend too much money on your remodel and the other expenses that go along with owning your home (like your mortgage, property taxes, insurance, and repairs), especially if you have other financial priorities.

Before you empty your bank account or commit to big debt and daunting monthly payments, think about your lifestyle. No matter how willing you think you are to make monetary sacrifices to change your home the way you want, you must ask yourself some questions: "Am I *really* going to stop going out to dinner or taking vacations?" Are those expensive haircuts, weekly manicures, and occasional shopping sprees necessities and not luxuries? It's as much an emotional thing as it is a business decision. You never want to spend more than you feel comfortable spending, no matter how much value you think you might be putting into your house.

A REALISTIC EQUATION:
Starting to Plan Your Budget

You may get information from a variety of sources—whether it's a magazine, website, or other source—about what a specific remodeling project will cost. But the truth is, every project is so different—from the details to the square footage and the cost of labor involved—that we think you are best served by learning about the methodology for planning a budget. If you follow the steps we give you, by the time a hammer hits a nail, you will have a much more accurate idea about what *your* project will cost than any study showing average costs could provide.

Planning the budget for your project is usually done in stages and you'll want to get preliminary estimates before the budget is fixed. There are many things to consider. Before you can set the fixed budget for your project, you will want to put together your remodeling wish list and get a rough idea—an estimate—of what each element is going to cost. Estimates will affect the decision to go ahead with certain work or not. Whether you have in mind an extreme makeover (like the complete room-by-room overhaul of a fixer), a simple nip/tuck (such as the renovation of one bathroom), or something in between, you will need to do some preliminary design planning so that the person with whom you are consulting will have at least an idea of what you have in mind.

Once you have gotten some estimates, you must take into account what we call the Oh-Nos!—the unexpected painful surprises that usually come up in a remodeling project that should be factored into the budget. We'll tell you more about that later in this chapter.

Finally, depending on what type of woman you are, you may also need to factor in the Might-as-Wells—the unanticipated impulse purchases or additions we make midstream to our remodel that give us so much pleasure but that cost us much more than we thought we would spend! Read on and you'll learn about these inevitable expenditures that become part of the equation as well.

GOING ALL THE WAY OR SAVING SOMETHING FOR LATER?

Remodels can be much like plastic surgery. There are many women who start out wanting their breasts done and then figure, while they're at it, they should go for the liposuction, too. One hospital room, one anesthesia, two procedures. The same mentality holds true for a home renovation. You might be tempted to make every change at once. For example, as long as you are remodeling the kitchen, why not fix up the bathroom? After all, you'll need to have a plumber, electrician, carpenter, and painter for both projects. There is an economy of scale to doing several or many projects at the same time. You'll usually save at least some money getting it all done at once.

Of course, you may not be able to afford the time, money, or major disruption to your life to do everything all at the same time. The decision to go all the way or save something for later is a very personal one—you will need to take into account your financial situation as well as your personal circumstances.

MAKING MISTAKES WHEN YOU REMODEL IN A RUSH

It is remarkable how many people don't do enough legwork at the outset and hastily dive into their project to their detriment. This often happens when someone is in a rush.

The Rushed Remodeler

There are many reasons why people rush their remodels: Maybe there is a new baby on the way, or they want to have that new kitchen and great room finished before the end of the summer. Sometimes, they are simply impatient. But the most common profile of the Rushed Remodeler is the one who is renovating a newly purchased home and needs to get all the work done by her move-in date. It could be that she and her husband need to get their kids settled into the new home before school starts or that she has sold her old home and has nowhere else to live. Whatever the situation, she mistakenly believes that advance planning will delay her move-in date without realizing that, although the legwork may delay the actual start of work, even the most rudimentary of plans can make things go a whole lot faster and more smoothly.

It is the Rushed Remodeler who often does not take the time to get a handle on costs in advance and who finds herself in sticker shock when the bills start rolling in:

Marci and her husband, Billy, bought a cute two-bedroom house in the suburbs. The house had a lot of character but, with a second child along the way, it wasn't big enough. The plan was to add on a family room, a third bedroom, and a third bathroom before moving in. Everyone warned Marci and Billy that renovations always take longer than initially planned, so with the lease on their city apartment running out in seven months, they found a contractor and got to work. They did just enough planning to get a permit for work to start. But they didn't do much planning for other critical details. Although the couple knew how much square footage they wanted to add, they weren't sure about most of the other details or finishes—they just assumed they would figure these things out and discuss costs with their contractor as they went along. With all their attention focused on getting started, they had their contractor begin construction without having any bids or even any cost estimates for many of the details and finishes. When the framing was done, it was time to make some more decisions. Marci and Billy didn't think the prices quoted per square foot for hardwood flooring for the downstairs and stone for their bathroom sounded so bad. The truth is, they didn't have any idea what it would all add up to or that they would have to pay for installation on top of it. And, to make matters worse, they didn't have a handle on many of the other costs of the project as well. By the time bills started rolling in, they were kicking themselves for not planning better. On top of everything, because they hadn't planned in advance, there were several delays in scheduling critical work and ordering materials that they should have purchased earlier. The whole reason they rushed—to save time—had backfired. Now they were emptying their savings account and were faced with living in an unfinished house at just the time the new baby was about to arrive.

MAKING PLANS AND HAVING DESIGNS ON YOUR PROJECT:
Preliminary Plans, Specifications, and Drawings

Certainly with a remodel that is extensive, and in an effort to avoid some of the problems we discussed in the last section, hiring the right design professional to draw up preliminary plans will be the first step toward getting a handle on costs. And even for a smaller project, having a simple plan drawn up can be very helpful in getting estimates.

Plans for Big Projects

You may have heard the term *plans and specifications* (or plans and specs). This term refers to the various design and other documents that architects and designers prepare to conceptualize and visualize the project for the owner; to show the contractor how to build; and to illustrate for everyone the materials, fixtures, appliances, and finishes that will be used. Architects prepare drawings in stages: They do preliminary drawings showing the basic ideas of the design for the project before construction begins and, later, draft documents that will have enough detail for the building department to issue a permit and for the contractor to bid and build the project.

On larger projects, the architect might do two different preliminary designs: schematic designs, which lay out the basic floor plan, followed by design development documents, which refine the design and add more detail (see Chapter 10). At each stage, the owner reviews and approves these designs in consultation with the architect to make sure things are on the right track. On larger projects, you might have a set of master plans, along with a separate set of plans for electrical, plumbing, utilities, or heating, ventilation and air-conditioning (HVAC). For example, electrical plans will show the location of the service entrance, meter, main circuit box, and circuits.

> ### Keeping Things in Check!
>
> On a big project, make sure you discuss with your architect the idea of getting periodic cost estimates during the various design phases to make sure he or she is drawing a house you can afford to build.

Plans for Small Projects

You may not think you need or want help on the design for a smaller project. You may not think you can afford it. We recommend that you think again. Even if you are just going to renovate a single room, it might be that you can't afford *not* to hire a design professional. You don't have to spend a fortune to have someone do a simple plan for your small job—and good advance planning will almost certainly save you time, money, and aggravation during the later stages of your remodel. A space planner or interior designer can be particularly helpful in showing you how to make the best use of limited space, configuring the different elements of each room being remodeled, and drawing your attention to things you might not have thought about.

Thinking About the Furniture

It's never too early to start thinking about how you will set up your remodeled space or to have someone help you with a simple furniture plan. It will help you plan certain details such as where you need wall and floor outlets.

The value of hiring a designer or space planner for a small project is clear from Judy's experiences with her small kitchen remodel.

Judy recently purchased a starter home that was small but cozy, charming, and had a lot of potential. A little work to the kitchen could make it the centerpiece of her home and increase its resale value. A self-described chef, subscriber to Architectural Digest, *and avid HGTV viewer, Judy felt she knew everything there was to know about creating the cook's kitchen of her dreams. But when she started shopping for appliances, looking at cabinetry, and considering countertops, she realized that she didn't know the first thing about putting it all together. Judy couldn't afford to spend a lot of money on this remodel and thought hiring a designer was an unnecessary expense—after all, this was her first house— but her best friend from college convinced her to buy a few hours of a designer's time. What a good investment that turned out to be! Heather, who had designed a few rooms for Judy's next-door neighbor, understood immediately just what Judy had in mind and drew a simple plan that brought the whole kitchen together. The plan included actual measurements for the placement of appliances—something Judy hadn't even focused on. Heather also helped Judy see how certain things worked better than others. For example, Judy had her heart set on a center island in the middle of her kitchen. Heather pointed out that an island would make the kitchen seem cramped—and the right cabinetry and well-placed countertops could solve the storage and work-space problems in a way an island never could. Judy would also save the cost of a new island. Armed with a simple plan, measurements, and a dose of reality, Judy could now start getting some estimates from contractors and pricing out cabinetry, countertops, and appliances in preparation for her remodel.*

Make Sure It Fits!

Sometimes the most impor- tant reason to have a simple plan prepared is to get accurate measurements of your space. There is nothing worse than ordering appliances, cabinetry or furniture, only to find that they don't fit.

Hiring your own designer or space planner isn't the only way to plan a smaller remodel. Many warehouse stores or specialty houses have designers on staff that can help you draw simple plans and prepare accurate measurements, particularly for kitchen and bathroom projects. And as we discuss in Chapter 7, there are also design/build firms that both design the project as well as implement the construction.

SO, WHAT'S THIS GOING TO COST?
Getting Preliminary Cost Estimates

Once you have plans or preliminary drawings, you will want to obtain cost estimates. Now let's get clear on what we mean here, because terminology is very important: *A cost estimate is not a bid.* A cost estimate is simply a rough projection of the potential costs based on rough plans or ideas. Contractors can give cost estimates at the preliminary stages of a remodel, when the plans aren't set but when the homeowner needs to establish approximately how much money the project is going to cost. By contrast, a bid is a commitment from a contractor to build whatever is itemized in the bid for the specified price; particularly for a large remodel, you may not be able to get a bid until you are in a more advanced stage of your planning. (We discuss the bidding process in Chapter 8.)

There are a number of ways to get cost estimates. One way is to bring in a reputable contractor to look over and discuss your plans. This does not have to be the contractor you will ultimately hire for the job—you should not commit to the contractor at this stage (see Chapter 7).

Do Not Sign a Cost Estimate

*I*f you sign a cost estimate, it can be interpreted as a binding contract with the contractor. If any contractor tries to get you to sign an estimate, refuse to do so.

Communicating Your Budget Limitations

When you sit down with a professional to get an idea of what your project will cost—whether it is a contractor or other professional—it is a good idea to speak frankly about the budget you have in mind, even if you are uncomfortable talking about money.

Many people think that if they give the contractor a budget, it will taint the contractor's estimates. They are afraid that the contractor will either inflate the estimate because he knows they can spend a certain amount or will make an estimate fit within the stated budget in an effort to get the job. Holding back essential information will not necessarily weed out unscrupulous or unprofessional contractors and it will usually prove to be counterproductive. (As we discuss in Part II, choosing your contractor wisely will be your key to avoiding someone who is dishonest.) Now, we are not suggesting compulsive oversharing or giving the person too much information—you certainly do *not* need to let anyone know how much money you have coming in each month or what you have in the bank. But it is a good idea to have a conversation about your contemplated budget and any budgetary limitations.

Other Ways to Find Out What Things Cost

In addition to bringing in a professional to get cost estimates, do your own homework to find out what things cost. Talk to friends who have remodeled their homes. You may feel awkward about asking them point blank how much they spent. But if you mention that you're thinking of remodeling but have no idea how much everything costs, you may get an outpouring of information and some frank talk about the numbers. You should also take some field trips. Check out kitchen design stores, where you can compare styles and prices for counters and cabinetry. Visit an appliance dealer or your local department store and start looking into the cost of appliances. Ask your best friend where she got that fabulous tile she just installed—and then go to the store to look at samples. Surf the Net. Be savvy and educate yourself.

REALITY SETS IN:
Factoring in Additional Costs You May Not Have Thought Of

You may have started this process having no clue about what your project was really going to cost, especially when each item taken alone doesn't seem that expensive. Brace yourself: The costs will probably add up in a big way. If you get realistic cost estimates, you may be shocked. You will probably be looking at numbers that are higher than you expected—rarely are things cheaper than you thought they would be. This is not, however, your ultimate moment of truth; there are still other things you need to add to the equation.

Extra Living Expenses

If you already own your home, you must determine if you will stay or move out during construction. Sometimes the decision to move out is made for you—if you are completely gutting your home, you simply can't live there. But if you are doing something less, then it is all a matter of tolerance and cost. Some people can live in a house without a kitchen (and love the idea of eating out every night), whereas others cannot and would not be able to stand the noise, dust, and disruption.

If you will need to move out or if you just purchased the home you are renovating and need to live somewhere else while the work gets done, you will need to factor this into your budget. Take into account double mortgage payments if you own another home or rent if you have to lease, moving and storage expenses, kennel costs for any pets that can't stay with you, utility bills, and the incidental costs of setting up a temporary household.

Remodeling a New Home and Selling an Old One?

If you have just bought a new home and have sold or are planning to sell your old one, you may want to try to remain in the place, either by extending the escrow period or by leasing back the home from the new owner. Extending the contract/escrow period is not always practical—you might need the money from your old place to pay for your new one—and postponing the closing is risky because the buyer can still back out of the deal until you transfer title. Oftentimes you are better off selling your old home and leasing it back as your buyer's tenant. Keep in mind that this has related costs of which you may not be aware. The buyer will probably want you to pay monthly rent and, if you sold the home for more than you paid for it, that rental payment will likely be more than the monthly payments you were making before you sold the home. This is because the typical buyer wants rental payments that are at least equal to the buyer's principal, interest, taxes, and insurance (PITI). In addition, the buyer may want a premium for letting you stay in the home.

One more thing: Most remodels fall behind schedule. So if you have just bought the home you are remodeling, even if you are able to stay in your old home for what you think is sufficient time to complete your remodel, it might not be long enough. You may be forced to move twice. Consider the story of Stephanie and Bryan:

> Stephanie and Bryan found a charming traditional house that had a lot of potential, but it had been neglected by its previous owners. They snatched it up for a great price and immediately got to work on their remodel. They put their old house on the market, and sold it in no time. They leased back their old house from the buyer for six months based on their contractor's assurances that their remodel would take no more than five. They were thrilled at the prospect of having so much time to remodel their new house before they had to move out of their old one.

Six months came and went in a flash, and their contractor told them that work on the new house was at least three months from completion. Forced to move from their old house, they had no choice but to lease an apartment for themselves and their three young boys. They didn't have many options: They needed a month-to-month arrangement on the apartment (since they didn't know how long they were going to need to stay), which meant that their monthly rent was higher than it would have been had they been able to sign a long-term lease. And three bedroom apartments aren't cheap. They ended up having to board their two large dogs since the apartment building didn't allow pets. They also had to store their belongings and pay to move twice (once from their old house to the apartment, and again from the apartment to the new house). And they had all the incidental expenses of setting up yet another household. These costs added up fast, and Stephanie hated having to spend money that could otherwise have gone toward new furniture. She also resented the inconvenience and disruption to their lives.

Oh-No! Expenses

Oh-Nos! are those unexpected (and often expensive!) unwelcome surprises that come up from time to time. They are the problems you didn't count on, like when your car unexpectedly breaks down and it ends up costing a bundle: You know the car needs to be fixed but you hate to spend the money, and you are at the mechanic's mercy because you have no idea how much the repairs should cost. It's the same with a home renovation: Even if you carefully plan and budget and get detailed cost estimates and even if your contractor provides a detailed and realistic bid, there are

---

Making the Contractor Pay

Some delays such as those due to bad weather are unavoidable. But your contract can make your contractor responsible for delays *he* causes that postpone the project beyond the agreed-upon completion date. You may be able to anticipate and put in the contract the extra costs to you of not having the project completed on time, like additional rent and boarding animals.

always surprises, emergencies, mistakes, and problems that come up. Dealing with the Oh-Nos! is going to cost you money—sometimes lots of it—but preparing for these glitches can make the sticker shock easier to handle.

Ideally, you should set aside an amount that is anywhere between 10 to 25 percent of your budget. We know this is painful to hear, especially if your budget is already tight. But it is much more painful to run out of money if you run into an unanticipated problem. The upside is that you could be lucky and *not* encounter too many Oh-Nos!, which means you can save some money for a rainy day . . . or, better yet, you can use it for some much-deserved Might-as-Wells!

Setting Aside a Little Extra

*I*t's a good idea to talk to your contractor about how much he would recommend setting aside for unanticipated costs. The amount the contractor comes up with will depend a lot on the age and condition of your home and nature of your remodel.

Might-as-Well Expenses

Might-as-Wells are the unanticipated pleasant impulse purchases that we all make from time to time. For example, you've just tried on the most fabulous pair of shoes. Sure, they cost way more than you wanted to spend . . . but they look so great, and they're so comfortable. You know you'll wear them and you'll love seeing them in your closet . . . might as well buy them in all four colors! And you might as well buy that skirt and top that go so perfectly, too!

It's no different when shopping for your remodel: You might find yourself saying, "Might as well get those antique knobs I want—even if they'll cost me three times more than the ones at the hardware store" or "Might as well install surround sound in the bedroom, as long as the walls are open." Really, how many times are you going to buy all new appliances? You might as well go for every top-of-the-line appliance you've ever dreamed of, starting with that Sub-Zero refrigerator!

Unlike Oh-Nos!, which come from life's little misfortunes and cost you money you hate to spend, Might-as-Wells are all about seizing opportunities and treating yourself—they are the little (or the huge) splurges that make you feel good. So every time you look at that spectacular refrigerator from across the room, you will feel a little pang of pleasure!

Sometimes, the trauma of Oh-Nos! can lead you to the fun of a Might-as-Well:

> Margo had always hated the linoleum in her bathroom and wanted that beautiful tile she had fallen in love with ever since she spotted it at that pricey tile store downtown. The rest of her bathroom was nothing special, with its ordinary fixtures, but she had been resisting remodeling it because she thought it would cost too much money and be too much trouble. The tile, she thought, would be enough. But when her tile guy ripped out that linoleum—oh no!—he discovered that the entire subfloor was soaking wet and rotted; the culprit was a leaky corroded pipe. Although the whole thing was going to be expensive, Margo soon realized she was lucky that the problem came to light when it did. More pipes could have leaked or burst without her ever discovering them, eventually causing a major mold or foundation problem. Now faced with extensive plumbing repairs— not to mention carpentry work on a new floor—Margo had to rethink everything. "It was a blessing in disguise," she said. "Since I had to do some major plumbing repairs anyway, I was going to have to open up a lot of walls, so I figured I might as well move a few things around the way I wanted them, and get all new bathroom fixtures while I was at it!" As it turned out, the old sink and tub would have looked tired next to Margo's gorgeous new tile. And an added bonus for Margo was that she ended up getting a great deal on her fixtures. An Oh-No! had not just become a Might-as-Well, it had become a fabulous remodeling opportunity.

TAKING IT TO THE BANK:
How to Pay for It

There are a lot of different ways you can finance your home renovation, and in this section we summarize some common ways to do so. You should speak with your banker, loan broker, accountant, or financial adviser to figure out a plan that works best for you.

Paying with Cash

The advantages of paying for your remodel with cash are clear: You won't be going into debt and you won't be paying interest on borrowed money. The disadvantages are just as clear: You might be house rich but you could make yourself cash poor—and it is never fun to empty your bank account. Even if you pay by cash, you can still sign up for a home equity loan just in case you ever need the money. You may never borrow a cent, and it usually costs little or nothing to keep the line of credit open on your home.

Loans Secured by Your Property

Most people buy homes and often finance construction on homes by borrowing money and then putting up the home itself as collateral for the repayment of the loan by giving the lender a mortgage or a deed of trust on the property. The lender is protected if the borrower stops making payments by being able to foreclose on the home—that is, get the loan repaid by selling the home and taking the amount owed to the lender from the proceeds. A lender will determine if you qualify for this kind of loan, not only by approving your credit and checking to see if you earn enough money to make your monthly payments, but also by determining whether your property's value sufficiently exceeds the amount of the loan and other liens affecting it. Construction loans, permanent loans, and home equity lines, as well as the conventional mortgage

The Cost of Money

Whenever you borrow money, remember that your credit will determine how much money you can borrow, the interest rate, or even whether the lender will lend to you at all. You also should make sure your lender or loan broker discloses all the fees, in addition to "points" (a percentage of the loan payable when the loan closes). There can also be loan origination fees, escrow and title insurance fees, lawyer fees, and appraisal fees, to name a few. You must factor these financing costs into your overall budget.

you get to buy your home, all fall into this category. Getting this kind of secured real estate loan could have tax benefits for you as a borrower; check with your financial adviser to see if you can deduct the mortgage interest and other costs from your taxes.

Construction Loans

A construction loan is a real estate loan specifically designed for financing the building or renovation of your home and is secured by a mortgage or deed of trust on your property. It's a little tricky from the lender's point of view because the lender is lending you money secured by something you haven't built yet. The lender will take extra care to make sure the property will be worth enough to cover repayment of the loan should the lender need to foreclose if you don't repay it. So, in addition to approving your credit, the lender will also usually want to approve the plans for the project, and sometimes the contract you enter into with your contractor. The lender will also not disburse the whole amount of the loan all at once. Instead, because the lender wants to make sure the loan is used for the construction project, it will make disbursements as needed to make progress payments to the contractor and to pay for other costs of the project (such as permit fees or the architect's bills). The lender usually approves these costs before they are paid, and the contractor's and other bills are often paid directly by the lender; the money may never pass through your hands at all. The lender will typically not pay until materials are delivered and the work described in the bill is completed. This isn't necessarily a bad thing—to some extent the lender is keeping an eye on your contractor! But remember, the lender is looking after its own interests, which are not necessarily the same as yours, so you can't depend on the lender to watch out for the things you care about. That's still your job.

Like the mortgage you obtained to buy your home, the construction loan is secured by a mortgage on your home. Since it is a mortgage on improvements that aren't built yet, the interest rate will generally be higher than interest rates for other types of real estate financing. When construction is over, your construction loan is usually replaced by permanent or take-out financing.

Permanent or Take-Out Financing

If you have a construction loan, once construction is completed, you will get what is known as a permanent loan that will take out—that is, pay off—the construction loan. Remember, the interest rate on a construction loan is higher than other types of financing because it is a loan secured by something that isn't built yet. So when construction is done, you will get a loan at a lower interest rate that is more like the kind of mortgage you get when you buy your home. You will often negotiate the construction loan and the permanent loan at the same time. Make sure you talk with your lender or financial adviser about how this fits into your financial plans. Permanent financing, like the mortgage you got when you bought your home, can have a fixed or variable interest rate. With a fixed-rate loan, interest is fixed throughout the term of the loan; whereas on an adjustable-rate loan, the interest rate varies at set intervals, depending on fluctuations of interest on a particular index. With a fixed rate loan, you know what you're getting yourself into and you know what your payments will be every month for the duration of the loan, but you will pay a higher interest rate at the outset for this certainty. With an adjustable-rate loan, you will pay less in interest at the outset, but any increases in market interest rates will cause the interest rate on the loan—and therefore your payments—to go up.

Home Equity Loan

A home equity loan is secured by your home. You may have heard people talking about getting cash for some purpose by "using the equity in their home." They usually mean that they are taking out a home equity loan, also called a home equity line of credit.

The difference between the total value of your property and the amount of debt against it is called the equity. If you have owned your home for a while, it has probably gone up in value and you can borrow money against the increase. Because home prices have risen quickly in the last few years, this has become one of the most popular ways of financing home improvements. Like your mortgage or your construction loan, this type of loan is also secured by your home, so the interest might be tax deductible.

Payments on a home equity loan are typically interest only for the term of the loan (usually about ten years), with the principal amount due at the end of the loan term. If you want to pay the principal off faster, there is usually no penalty for doing so. Interest rates on home equity lines of credit are usually variable, so as market interest rates change, so will the interest rate on the home equity line. Depending on interest rates at the time you obtain your loan, rates for home equity lines may be higher or lower than interest rates for other types of loans. Still, the rates might be lower than on construction loans, and you can pay this type of loan off sooner than you could a permanent loan. Another advantage to this type of loan is that you can use the loan proceeds for whatever you want—your remodel, a new car, or your kid's education—and the lender will have no say over how you spend the money at all. If you are seeking to obtain a home equity loan to finance your remodel, you will need to obtain your loan before construction begins.

5

Getting to Know Your Home Inside Out Before You Remodel:

A PRIMER OF THE MOST COMMON REPAIRS AND UPGRADES

*R*EGARDLESS OF WHETHER you've been with your home for a while and need to spice things up or you've recently met and are first building a life together, there are certain things that every woman should know about her home's attributes before remodeling. If you can spot your home's flaws and limitations ahead of time, you'll know what you'll need to work on and what renovations will and won't be possible.

Your home may have certain problems that you aren't aware of. Now is the time to learn about them so that you run into as few unwelcome surprises down the road as possible. Also, like all things in life, there may be things you've swept under the rug. Since you're hiring a contractor anyway, you might as well fix those annoyances you've been trying to ignore.

In this chapter, we tell you about your home's systems (like electricity and plumbing), scary stuff that you could

Avoiding Those Oh-Nos!

As we've said, if you are not careful (and even if you are), remodeling has the potential for a lot of Oh-No! moments. "Oh no! I just wanted to add a spa tub to my master bath, but now my plumber is telling me I'd better do something about those corroded pipes we discovered when we opened the walls!" "Oh no! My contractor says my house doesn't have enough power for my state-of-the-art media room and appliances and I need a new panel and major electrical work!" What's a woman to do? While there is no magic formula for avoiding every Oh-No! moment, getting to know your home better *before* you start remodeling will certainly help you discover them and plan in advance.

find in the walls, and many other important things you'll need to know about. If you are remodeling a co-op, condo, or home in a planned community, be sure to read the last sections in this chapter, which apply to your unique situation.

You may be asking yourself "Why should I read about all this stuff if I have a contractor working for me? Won't he let me know about any problems with my home?" The answer is, don't count on it! You can expect your contractor to focus only on the work you say you want to have done. And, while your contractor might spot a problem that will affect the work, there may be other things that you should or will want to deal with now. Of course, we're not here to teach you how to do the work yourself so we don't need to get too technical. But we will give you just enough information so that you'll know what to discuss with your remodeling team.

The Key Questions

There are four key questions you'll need to ask—and get answers to—before you begin your remodel.

- **Is it in good shape?** Let's face it: Things break or wear out. Remodeling is a good opportunity to get to the bottom of (and fix) whatever is causing that crack in the wall, leaky faucet, or other minor irritation—or major defect—you've been living with.

- **Is it dangerous?** As you are discussing your remodeling plans and ideas with your contractor, and even if you are planning to remodel just a small portion of your home, ask your contractor to advise you about any unsafe or potentially unsafe conditions lurking in your home. It could be that something wasn't built or installed properly; is simply old, outdated, and worn out; or doesn't meet current safety standards. Common safety risks include faulty wiring or hazardous substances in the home (like asbestos). Don't be cheap or sloppy when it comes to safety. Also consider hiring a licensed home inspector to conduct a physical inspection of your home before you remodel. We tell you more about that later in this chapter.

- **Is it breaking the law?** No matter how innocent your home may look, it could still be a law breaker! You'd be surprised

Beware of Funky Additions!

*Y*ou've always loved that enclosed patio (even if it's a little drafty and leaks when it rains), or that extra room with the kitchenette above your garage that you lease to that nice college student. But if other homes in your neighborhood don't have these features, you should be a little suspicious. Any unusual or below-par construction should make you take a closer look. Your drafty, leaky patio might have been enclosed without a permit, which is required in most locations. And the "single unit with kitchenette" may also be illegal; a lot of places that are zoned for single-family homes don't allow additional units on the property.

what a little detective work will uncover. You'll need to know if any prior work was done without obtaining the necessary permits or complying with applicable building codes. Your contractor should pull all the permits on your home to find out if proper permits were obtained for all the previous construction to your home. You might have to make certain changes to your home to bring it into compliance with building codes whether or not this was part of your original remodeling plan. You will also want to find out whether the changes you want to make will violate any laws or building codes. Your contractor will often be able to advise you on certain current code requirements off the top of his head. Local authorities issuing building permits will also be checking the construction and signing off on permits throughout your remodel.

- **Is this good enough?** Your home might be perfectly safe or comply with current codes, but you still might need or want to upgrade certain aspects of it to accommodate increased square footage or add certain amenities. For example, you might need to increase the number of amps of electricity to your home due to added features, like new air-conditioning or an ever-growing number of home appliances.

LET'S GET PHYSICAL:
The Benefits of Having a Home Inspection

You are probably wondering just how you go about learning what you need to know about your home. If you have recently purchased it, you probably had a professional home inspector conduct a comprehensive physical inspection of your home before you agreed to buy it. This inspector should have prepared a written report giving you a lot of information about your home: for example, the condition of the roof and your home's systems (plumbing; electrical; and heating, ventilation, and air-conditioning—HVAC), and any foundation problems that would cause concern. You should definitely give a copy of any written inspection report to your contractor, as well as any architect, designer, and engineer working on your project.

But if you've lived with your home for a while (or didn't do a thorough inspection of your new home), you may not have a handle on the condition of many of these things, and a lot may have changed since you and your home first got together. Although it is not that common to do a comprehensive physical inspection before remodeling a home you have owned for a while, getting one is not a bad idea, especially if your home is old and your remodel will be extensive. It will give you a lot of good information.

If you hire a home inspector, make sure the company is reputable and your home inspector is licensed (see Resources). Even though you will be getting a written report, make sure you are present for the inspection. You'll accomplish so much more when your inspector can point things out to you—and you will have the added bonus of being able to ask questions to your heart's content!

Whether you hire a home inspector or not, it is important that you know at least a little bit about your home's systems and structures—and what can affect them—so you can understand the repairs, replacements and remedies you might need to take care of during your remodel. You'll get a lot more out of your conversations with your contractor, and you'll impress him with your knowledge, too! Don't worry—we aren't going to overwhelm you with too much information but read the rest of this chapter to get a handle on the basics.

Getting It Over With

A remodel might be the right occasion to replace or upgrade some feature of your home if major repairs are in the not-too-distant future anyway. For example, even if your current pipes are doing the job, you might want to change them from galvanized steel to copper because you know if you leave them alone they won't last much longer. It can cost less money in the long run to have everything done all at once—and you won't have the aggravation or headaches of having your home invaded by workmen again!

ARE THERE SPARKS?
The Electrical System

Replacing Wiring

Your remodeled home will look hot when you're done with it but you want to make sure that your wires are not. If you are about to remodel an older home, be on the lookout for old wiring that you might need to replace. Certain types of wiring used before the early 1970s would never be installed today and should be replaced before becoming a fire hazard—if you don't have a fire hazard on your hands already. Consult with your electrician if there is a possibility that your wiring is old. There are other safety concerns that you'll need to watch out for. For example, a specific type of outlet called a ground fault interrupter (GFI) outlet should be installed and will probably be required by law for any kitchen or bathroom remodel; anywhere that an outlet is close to water. You have seen these outlets—they sometimes trip and don't work unless you press a button. Irritating, yes, but they are there to keep us from getting electrocuted.

Increasing Amp Capacity

Depending on how much electricity your newly remodeled home will use, you may need to increase the flow or amperes (amps) of electricity to the home. A typical three-bedroom, two-thousand-square-foot house should have at least a 100-amp capacity. For a larger home, you may even need as much as four-hundred amps or more.

Hooking Things Up, Plugging Things In, and Turning Things On

There are some design conveniences you should be looking at, too. If you are installing new light switches, make sure they are installed in a convenient location and at a height that you like. And, as we noted earlier, don't forget to make sure each room has enough plugs and hookups for cable television, computers, phones, home entertainment systems, and large appliances in the kitchen.

ARE THESE PIPES YOUR TYPE?
The Plumbing System

Pipe Pressure

What happens when you turn on all the faucets at once and flush the toilets in your home? If the flow to the tub or other faucets slows when you do this or the shower hits you with scalding or freezing water when the toilet flushes, you should talk to a plumber. It might indicate a serious problem, or it could just be a matter of adjusting the water pressure.

Replacing Pipes

There are a lot of different types of pipes that have been used in residential construction over the years. The ones in your home might have been there long enough to cause you problems—if not now, then soon. If you are going to install new plumbing, copper pipes are definitely the way to go. They last for fifty to seventy-five years and provide good water pressure.

If your home has older pipes, then they are probably made of galvanized steel. These pipes tend to wear out after about thirty to forty years, so even if everything seems fine, if you are doing any sort of major remodel, you may want to replace them now rather than waiting for the pipes to burst, the flow to become restricted, or brown water to start coming out of the faucet. It is common in a remodel to replace only those pipes that are exposed and leave the unexposed pipes untouched.

BITCHIN' BATHS AND SIZZLIN' SHOWERS:
Hot-Water Heaters

Hot-Water Capacity

Hidden in basements or special closets, hot-water heaters provide one of life's greatest yet most simple pleasures: hot running water for your shower or bath. Consult with your contractor or a plumber to make sure you will have enough hot-water capacity for your needs. There is nothing worse than having to rush out of the shower after being hit by a blast of cold water because the hot water has run out!

Heater Leaks

You should also make sure you have your hot-water heater checked out for leaks and age. Make sure you replace your hot-water heater before the end of its natural lifespan (which differs from heater to heater, but is typically ten years). Also, make sure your hot-water heater is *not* located on an upper floor of your home where, if it bursts, it will do more damage than if it is located on the first floor, in the garage, or in the basement.

RUNNING HOT AND COLD:
Heating, Ventilation, Air-Conditioning, and Insulation

Your HVAC Unit

If you are thinking of replacing your HVAC system, your contractor can advise you as to what type will work best in your home. As the single biggest user of energy in your home, your HVAC system can lead to huge bills in the summer for air-conditioning and in the winter for heating. That's why one of the most important things to discuss with your contractor is energy efficiency.

Insulation

Energy efficiency is not just about the furnace or air-conditioner. It is also about the insulation in your home that can keep the heat or cold generated by your system in and the elements out. If you've noticed a cool draft coming in from under a doorway or through a window when you're trying to heat the place or wondered why your current system just isn't keeping your home cool, make sure you discuss this with your contractor.

IS THERE A SOLID FOUNDATION HERE?
Foundations and Basements

Foundations

Your relationship with your home must be built on a solid foundation—literally! Foundation problems can be complex because they can involve both structural elements and soil conditions, so you'll want to talk with a specialist—such as a structural engineer, soils engineer, or a geologist—before you do any major structural work or if you suspect any problems. Your suspicions should be aroused if you see uneven flooring or stairs; cracks in the walls, ceilings, or foundation; and doors or windows that do not close snugly. A big warning sign is if a previous addition to the house is not at the same level as the original building. You should also be suspicious if you spot moisture around the foundation or detect an odd odor. But before you get nervous, find out if something is wrong by hiring the right specialist; these things could be signs that something is amiss with the foundation or could simply be the result of natural settling of the home. Settling isn't necessarily a bad or unexpected thing; in fact, most homes experience settling in the first few years after construction. However, a good contractor will tell you to hire an engineer who specializes in foundations to inspect and check out these potential warning signs and make any necessary recommendations.

Basements

If you are remodeling your basement and converting it into usable living space, you should have it checked out carefully first. The most important thing to look for is water intrusion: This could cause a mold problem. Go with your instincts: Musty smells and stains on the floors or panels can all be signs of water problems. Water can come from outside the basement or from leaky pipes. A soggy basement could be a sign of costly foundation problems, too.

A ROOF OVER YOUR HEAD:
Roofs and Gutters

New additions and second stories obviously require new roofing. But roofs in general can be a classic Might-as-Well: "Might as well replace the fifteen-year-old roof as long as there is so much work to do anyway." This makes a lot of sense if you've had a lot of leaks in the past or if the roof is in really bad shape.

Types of Roofs

There are many different types of roofing styles and materials. What you choose will probably depend on the style of your home as well as local building codes. You should also speak to your contractor about what type of roof your home can support if you need to replace the one you have. For example, you can't put heavy Spanish-style ceramic roofing or slate on just any home. Many homes would not be able to support the weight of this roofing material. You should also consider the fire resistance of the material. Building codes in some areas forbid certain roofing materials that are considered to be highly flammable.

Gutters

Chances are you have never given much thought to rain gutters, but these relatively inexpensive items can be critical to the preservation of your roof and your foundation. A good gutter system draws water off the roof and away from the foundation of the property. Your contractor, home inspector, or gutter installer can do a simple inspection of your home to see if your gutter system works. We can't underestimate how important gutters can be—water pooling at the base of the home can intrude into basements and crawl spaces, causing mold and possibly even compromising the foundation.

PLAYING WITH FIRE:
The Chimney and Fireplace

If you have an old fireplace and chimney, before you make a date for a romantic evening to snuggle up by the fire, there's another date you should make . . . with a licensed chimney inspector. Your inspector will tell you if your chimney is safe or whether any repairs are required, but here are a few things to keep in mind: A chimney should be capped to keep water out and should be covered with wire to make sure that little animals don't make themselves at home inside of it. Your inspector should also check the bricks and mortar of the chimney inside and out to make sure they don't need to be repaired and that there are no obstructions inside that could cause a fire. And keep in mind that the height and distance of wooden mantels and other parts of the fireplace may be regulated by the local building code—there may be things you'll be required by law to change once you start remodeling.

SCARY THINGS THAT MAKE US SCREAM:
Asbestos, Mold, and Other Frights

Asbestos

If you, your contractor, or your home inspector suspects that the home contains asbestos, you should consult with licensed professionals about inspecting and possibly removing it.

Asbestos can cause cancer if it is inhaled. It is most likely to be inhaled when it becomes airborne (or friable), and it generally becomes friable if it is disturbed. Some experts will advise leaving asbestos in place if it is in a sealed area, is not airborne, and will not be disturbed, because they believe that leaving the asbestos undisturbed is safer than risking releasing it into the air where it can be inhaled. You should consult with an asbestos inspection and removal company about the condition of any asbestos in your home.

Even if your inspection and removal company has deemed it safe to leave the asbestos undisturbed, there are many reasons you might want to have it removed in any case. For example, the heating systems of some old homes contain asbestos; this asbestos can eventually become airborne and therefore inhaled through a home's ventilation system. And asbestos in your home may be disturbed (and, therefore, become friable) as you do work on your home. See Resources for how to get more information on asbestos.

Toxic Mold

Toxic mold is the ghoulish house nightmare du jour. Part of the natural environment, mold is found in most indoor and outdoor spaces. It can be a problem if it grows uncontrolled indoors and/or if people with mold sensitivity are exposed to it. Most people are unaffected by molds, but molds can cause health problems such as allergic reactions or asthma attacks. Still, there is no consensus among experts how a particular mold might affect any given person.

Indoor mold growth can and should be prevented or controlled by limiting moisture indoors. If there is mold growth in your home, you will need to clean up the mold *and* fix the water problem. If you clean up the mold but don't fix the water problem, then, most likely, the mold problem will come right back.

If you suspect you have a mold problem, as part of your remodel, you should contact a licensed mold inspection and abatement company. Not only are there health concerns but you may also want to sell your home down the road and many buyers will not touch a house that has a mold problem.

Lead

Lead is toxic if breathed or ingested. The older the house, the more likely there will be lead somewhere in it. If you're aware of the presence of lead, you'll want to get rid of it immediately. Lead was used in pipe connections in older homes for many years. If those pipe connections are corroded, lead can enter the drinking water. This is dangerous and any pipes containing lead should be replaced.

Lead paint can also be a problem. Lead paint has been banned in the United States since 1978, and if your house was built before then, you could have lead paint on the walls. The only way you can tell if your paint contains lead is if you have it tested. (You can get a lab to test for lead, and there are also several home tests on the market.) If you will be scraping, sanding, or stripping walls as part of your remodel, the paint particles could become airborne and inhaled. You also want to be careful that children do not eat paint chips. There are companies that specialize in lead abatement—hire one if you have lead paint in your home.

EVERYBODY HATES BUGS:
Termites and Other Pests

If you have just bought the home you are remodeling, chances are the seller was required to have the property inspected for the presence of termites and other wood-destroying pests and to provide you with a report. If you have lived in your home for a long time, consider having a termite inspection done before you start remodeling. You can then deal with the repair of any damage caused by termites during your renovation. But it's a toss-up as to whether you should fumigate before or after you finish the construction work. On the one hand, if you fumigate after your remodel, then you can get rid of termites that could be present in new wood that is brought into the house during construction. On the other hand, getting the bugs out often involves tenting the whole house, which can damage the roof. Repair to the roof may not be something you want to address at the end of your remodel. Bring up the issue of when to tent your home with your contractor.

IT'S THE LAW, MA'AM:
Zoning and Building Codes

Zoning

Zoning laws and regulations govern things like whether a particular neighborhood is commercial or residential, the size of lots and buildings in neighborhoods, and height and other building restrictions for buildings and other structures. So, for example, if you want to increase the size of your home or add a second story, you will need to find out whether zoning laws will allow you to do this. Your contractor or architect (if you are working with one) should have general knowledge about these laws and codes and whether they'll affect your ability to make the changes you want to your house.

Suppose you want to make a change that is restricted by zoning requirements? Let's say you want to build an exterior wall that would be taller than zoning law permits. The only way to do that legally is to get the proper governmental authority to make an exception to the law for you—this is called a variance. Variances are often tough to get and sometimes the procedure for obtaining a variance involves getting the consent of your neighbors, so it always pays to be on good terms with them.

Building Codes

Building codes are a combination of state and local government requirements that regulate construction, primarily for public safety. Such codes relate to everything from the types of building materials permitted; standards for electrical, plumbing, or other systems; and requirements for building walls and foundations. There is usually no way around a building code requirement if you are building from the ground up or making major changes, such as building an addition or taking all or part of your house down to the studs. If you are not making such dramatic changes, you might have a little more leeway. There might be certain aspects of your home that do not comply with current code, but you can leave them alone without upgrading them if they are grandfathered because they were built in accordance with code requirements in effect when the work was done. Other existing parts of your home will have to be brought up to current codes, even if they were built to the codes in place at the time. (This is one of the ways you can be hit with unexpected costs.) Sometimes building codes are very clear about what must be done, and your contractor can tell you what he thinks must stay and what must be changed. Other times, codes can be rather vague, and the building inspector may have discretion to say what can stay and what must go. So when you meet your building inspector, make sure that you are nice and friendly; he has quite a bit of control over your destiny!

IN BED WITH A LOT OF PEOPLE AT ONCE:
Private Restrictions for Adjacent Property Owners, Condos, Co-ops, and Planned Communities

Restrictions

In addition to restrictions on property that may be imposed by the government, some homes in particular neighborhoods, planned communities, condominiums (condos), or co-operatives (co-ops) are subject to private restrictions and rules that can be enforced by other property owners, a board, or a committee. These restrictions will regulate things that affect your remodel, such as the style of home in a planned community or whether you can take down a wall or move a gas line in a condo.

The restrictions or rules that affect your remodel may be found in a document called "Covenants, Conditions, and Restrictions" (CC&Rs), articles and by-laws, house rules, and other documents that a homeowner should receive when she buys her property. Some buildings and communities will also have specific forms that outline the necessary steps one has to take when undertaking a renovation. Often, these guidelines will include a list of what documents must be submitted for approval. You can usually get this form from the managing agent of the property or community.

Most planned communities, condos, and co-ops also have boards of directors and/or architectural committees that have the power to approve or disapprove your plans. It's lousy to spend a lot of money on plans, only to find out that you can't do what you want because someone on the board or architectural committee has blackballed you. So it's never too early to start talking—and making friends—with the neighbors who will be approving your remodel.

It is also important to know that the relevant board or committee may also need to approve your general contractor and most likely will require him to be appropriately licensed and insured. So, your uncle, who does work on the side, but isn't a licenced contractor, may not be able to handle your renovation.

What Will the Building Take Care Of?

One of the most important and often confusing parts of living in a building with other homeowners is figuring out what things you are responsible for versus what things are the responsibility of the building. The governing documents will often have the answers. So, for example, if the building is responsible for the plumbing pipes in the walls and you are having water pressure problems, you might have to go through the building to get the repairs you need. This won't always be easy. Some homeowners' associations and

Condo or Co-Op?

You've probably heard the terms *condo* and *co-op* before and perhaps have wondered what the difference is. Actually, they are very similar—in both cases, the owners have the right to use their units as well as common areas in the building, such as elevators and hallways. The differences between the two are basically legal ones. An owner of a condominium actually owns real property; she owns her unit (and perhaps a parking space or two, or a storage unit). She also owns, along with the other owners of the building, the common areas. Co-ops are owned differently; a legal entity (such as a corporation) owns the building, and each owner owns stock or other shares in the entity. Each owner has a "proprietary lease" (that is, a lease that goes along with her shares) that gives her the exclusive right to use her unit for a very long term (for example, one hundred years). This lease is renewed periodically. The proprietary lease may also give her the right to use certain limited common elements of the building (for example, a portion of the roof garden) that are specifically assigned to her unit, as well as the same right that all the other owners in the building have to use the common areas. For all practical purposes, a co-op owner's rights are the same as those of an owner of a condo, and she can remodel her unit so long as she gets the required approval.

boards are quite organized and managed well (especially in buildings with a large number of units), whereas others—typically those with few units—may be less organized and helpful. Make sure you read all the applicable documents and speak to the managing agent or head of the board before you start any work.

6

Is It Worth It?
YOUR REMODEL AS AN INVESTMENT

THERE ARE A lot of factors that go into figuring out whether remodeling will be a good investment. There is investing in your home as an asset, and there is investing in your remodel for your personal enjoyment. Of course, you would like to see your home go up in value even if you have no plans to sell it in the immediate future. After all, it's probably your biggest asset. Betting that your remodel will increase your home's value is also a great way to rationalize spending all that money! But don't assume that the changes you contemplate make financial sense. Learn the things you need to know to make that determination.

IS THIS HOME HUSBAND OR BOYFRIEND MATERIAL?

As is the case with any new romance, before you commit to putting a lot into your home, you should ask yourself how long you see this lasting. If your home is husband material and you think you will be together for a long time, then it may not be quite as important to you that every change you make adds something to the resale value of the home. You know that you'll be enjoying the changes you make for a long time and there's a lot of value in that.

If your home is just boyfriend material and you see yourself being together for only a few more years at most, then you are probably thinking more in terms of what you will be left with when you move on.

Either way, you'll probably want to have some idea about how the dollars you spend on your remodel will affect the value of your home.

VALUE ADDED

"How much value will my remodel add to my home?" When you ask yourself this question, what you really want to know is how much you could sell your home for after it's been remodeled

Is Everyone Flipping Out over "Flipping"?

Flipping is the ultimate fling—you and your home are together for a short time, you fix it up, and then you part ways with a lot of extra money in your pocket, you hope. If you have bought a home as an investment only, whether you'll hold it for a while or put it right back on the market, then, obviously, your remodel will not be about your personal enjoyment. You'll be concerned only with how much value the renovations will add to the home. There are people who do this for a living, hopping around from house to house, but it can be risky and it is not for everyone.

compared to how much it would go for before you remodel it. Since real estate markets fluctuate, the best you can do is to try to figure this out in present time. This isn't an exact science because there are so many factors that affect what the individual buyer will pay.

It is generally accepted by experts in the remodeling industry that updating kitchens and bathrooms adds the most value. But even with remodeled kitchens and bathrooms, you can't assume that you will get back 100 percent of what you spent on your remodel when you go to sell your home. It is true that in hot markets, however, certain improvements may add

The Up-and-Coming Neighborhood

A fixer home in an up-and-coming neighborhood can be a smart investment if you are one of those people who has a good sense of what is going on in your area. As prices go up, suddenly your fixer home—all fixed up—in a marginal neighborhood will be the fabulously renovated dream home in the now-hot neighborhood that is the envy of all your family and friends. And you will surely earn their admiration by having gotten in early!

more than 100 percent of their cost to the value of the home. This is why flipping becomes so popular in hot markets. In more moderate markets, though, you will need to temper your expectations about how much more value your remodel will add to your home.

There are several local and national surveys that have compiled statistics of cost-versus-value ratios: comparisons of the average cost of different types of remodels to the value these changes add to the average home (see Resources). Keep in mind that these raw numbers don't say it all. There are also a lot of other factors to consider.

Location

Home values vary greatly from location to location. The average three-bedroom home in Beverly Hills may cost three to four times more than a comparable home in Oklahoma City. So you don't want to rely solely on some national survey—no matter how reputable—to figure out whether you are truly adding value. Look at reports that are broken down city by city.

An even more important resource can be looking at the recent comparable sales (comps) of homes in your area because it will give you a more accurate idea of what is going on locally. You can speak with a real estate agent who specializes in home sales in your neighborhood to get this information. Look at the features of nearby homes—from size to the different kinds of rooms—to get an idea (both before and after) of what your home is worth now and what it may be worth after you remodel it.

Popularity and Trends

One thing to keep in mind is that you will get the most bang for your buck and add the most value to your home, dollar for dollar, when your renovation includes the most popular types of additions, upgrades, and changes. Think about it: If you live in a neighborhood that families with children want to live in, then adding a great room or other family-friendly amenity will appeal to a lot more buyers. If you add something that is not so family-friendly to a home in a family neighborhood—like a fancy dining room instead of a third bedroom—then you'll have fewer prospective buyers since the house won't appeal to the majority of people who wish to move to that area.

And don't forget about trends. Improvements that are hot when you remodel are often a good investment if you sell right away. There are a number of home design trend surveys that will clue you in to what remodeling projects are the most popular at a particular time (see Resources for trend reports).

The Best Home in the Neighborhood Is Usually Not a Good Investment

You may have heard that you never want to buy the best house—the largest, fanciest, or most expensive—in the neighborhood. The most expensive house on the block brings up the value of all the others, but the less expensive ones bring down the values of the better ones. So keep in mind that any high-end renovations you make (such as adding a media room or wine cellar) might not add the same value if your home is in a modest neighborhood than it would if you had made these changes to a residence that is surrounded by fancier homes in a swankier ZIP code. Similarly, if you add a fourth bedroom to a home in a neighborhood where all the homes have two to three bedrooms, you may not find your home goes up as much in value. Sure, your home might sell for a little more than the one down the street; however, you won't be adding as much value as you think. Add that fourth bedroom to a home where most of the homes in the neighborhood have four to five bedrooms, and you may see a bigger difference.

Other Renovations That May Boost Your Home's Value

Besides kitchens and bathrooms, there are several other kinds of renovations that can make a big difference in how potential buyers perceive your home and, therefore, how much they'll be willing to pay for it:

- **The front lawn and driveway.** You've probably heard the term *curb appeal*. This means the first impression someone gets of your house when approaching it. If you have a house, the front lawn and driveway are probably the first things that people see. There's a lot you can do to improve their appearance. Landscaping, fixing, or replacing worn pathways and patios, and fixing a cracked or stained driveway are all things to consider. You should also know that many buyers come back at night for another look. A nicely lit front lawn makes a home look inviting at night.

- **The entryway.** In any home—whether it is a house, co-op, or condo—the entryway is important. If your home does not have a separate and distinct entryway that is set apart from the rest of the house, consider adding or creating one. You can make even a small entryway stand out.

- **Refinishing old floors and painting the walls.** The condition of your floors and walls makes a huge impact on how buyers will rate the overall condition of your home. Regrouting old tile floors, refinishing hardwood floors, replacing stained carpeting, and adding a fresh coat of paint can make all the difference.

- **Replacing old-fashioned light switches and old hardware.** You wouldn't think that such small details matter, but things like those old up and down light switches and doorknobs that are in bad shape are a signal to a buyer that the home has not been updated, and this can drag down the price of your home. Distinguish hardware and light switches that are in bad shape from beautiful vintage details that many homeowners and home buyers may find very appealing.

YOU'RE WORTH IT!

Before you abandon plans to makeover your home because you don't think the changes will increase its value, think again. There is also such a thing as investing in yourself, especially if you are going to live in the home for quite a long time and will have many years to enjoy it. You just need to keep in mind that any unusual or unconventional change you make might not be so popular with the average buyer when you go to sell your home. But you might just end up saying to yourself, "Who cares? *I'm* worth it!"

Hiring and Handling the Right People for the Job

7

The New Man in Your Life:
HOW TO CHOOSE THE RIGHT GENERAL CONTRACTOR

THERE IS NO one more important on your team than your general contractor. Hiring the right man for this job is the single most important thing you can do to set your remodel up for success.

You and your general contractor will be spending a lot of time together. This will not be a casual relationship! You may see him first thing in the morning before you blow-dry your hair, after a hard day at the office, or after a long day with the kids when you're feeling tired and cranky. Depending on your schedule, there are times when you may be spending all day together. So you need to find someone who you feel comfortable working with. Having a good rapport with each other will make your remodeling experience that much more successful and enjoyable. On the flip side, if you feel annoyed or intimidated by a contractor's personality, you'll have a miserable time. Just remember though, it's got to be much more than a feel-good type of thing. So while he may be charming when you meet him, the right man for the job must have a lot of other things going for him, and you will have to check him out carefully.

In this chapter and the next, we tell you everything you ever wanted to know about hiring a general contractor but were afraid to ask. We clue you in to all the things a general contractor does (or should be able to do), and we show you how to select one. We walk you through how to interview contractors and check their credentials and references. By the time you're finished reading, you'll know exactly what you should be looking for and when you should run in the opposite direction as fast as you can! Although we don't go into detail about your contract with him until Chapter 9, we want to put

> it out there right now that you do need to have one. (Yes, this relationship requires a prenuptial agreement of sorts!) Finally, we give you some critical female advice on how to get this very important new relationship off to a good start.

> ### Your New Mantra
>
> *I* will have a written contract, I will, I will!

YES, HE'S OUT THERE!

It's true, a good general contractor is hard to find, but he is out there, even though it may seem like all the good ones are taken. And it's also true that there are a lot of losers, too. Let's face it, we've all heard the horror stories: the heartbreaking tale of the contractor who runs out on some poor woman with all her money smack in the middle of her remodel. The alarming anecdotes of schedules and budgets spiraling out of control. Tales of terror of mismanagement and botched jobs. In fact, in this era of remodeling mania, it seems almost impossible to get through a day without hearing someone launch into a tirade about some rotten general contractor. And these cautionary tales are supported by some sobering statistics: Home improvement fraud ranks among the top complaints made to state attorneys' general offices year after year.

Fortunately, we are happy to report some good news: For all the incompetent or unscrupulous contractors out there, there are many highly professional, dependable, ethical contractors who will do a great job for you. Your man is out there, and we will show you how to find him!

THE GENERAL CONTRACTOR'S JOB DESCRIPTION

It takes a big man to be a general contractor. He should be experienced in virtually every aspect of renovating a home because he is responsible for coordinating and implementing your entire project. He must also have technical, business, and interpersonal skills and should have specific experience in handling your type of project. When you realize how extensive this job is, you will come to have great respect for the competent ones, and you will also understand why so many contractors are just not up to the task.

His Credentials

The contracting business is loosely regulated in some states and more stringently regulated in others; not every state requires general contractors to be licensed. But even if a license is required, it often means very little. A license really doesn't say anything about a contractor's abilities and certainly won't tell you anything about his integrity. One thing is for certain, though: If the state requires a license and a contractor doesn't have one, then you should *not* hire him. Someone who is not capable of meeting the minimum standards may very well have other problems in the way he runs his business. It indicates a lack of responsibility on his part. Also, some states have plans that will refund money to consumers who have certain types of problems with their contractors, but you may not be entitled to any financial reimbursement if you hire a contractor who has not met the state's licensing requirements. So find out if your state requires a contractor to be licensed (see Resources). If it does, record the license number and make sure it is still valid. If the contractor does not have one, just say no, and cross him off the list of potential candidates.

Subcontractors

Don't confuse a specialist—like an electrician, plumber, or carpenter—with a general contractor. A specialist probably doesn't have the ability to oversee an entire project unless he also happens to be a general contractor. In this book, we refer to these specialists as *subcontractors* (or *subs* for short), as *tradesmen*, or by their specialty (such as electrician, carpenter, and plumber). When we refer to the *contractor*, we are referring to the general contractor only and not to one of these specialists.

Typically you will hire your general contractor and he, in turn, will bring in the subcontractors for the job. This arrangement makes the general contractor ultimately responsible to you for the quality of the work of all the subs. The key benefit is that your general contractor will be responsible directly to you to construct, complete, and correct any work. You, on the other hand, will not have to engage or go after the individual subcontractor to finish the work or correct it if something goes wrong. This is especially helpful if problems involving more than one trade come up: It will be the general contractor's obligation—not yours—to track down and coordinate various trades to fix the problem.

Taking Care of Business

Your general contractor must also be a good businessman. He must be well organized to keep track of the details of your job. This is the only way he can maintain high quality while trying his best to stay on schedule and on budget. He must also pay his subcontractors and material suppliers on time. But it's not just about paperwork—your contractor must be a good manager of people so he can coordinate and manage the efforts of his subs and work well with the rest of your team. As is the case with any business, the personality of the person in charge can make all the difference in overall morale and, ultimately, overall quality. Subcontractors who are treated well and paid on time will be happier . . . and happy workers do a better job! Conversely, you and your soon-to-be beautiful home are in trouble if a general contractor is a poor businessman, lets the details get away from him, fails to pay subs or material suppliers on time (or not at all), or treats people poorly.

Can You Be Your Own General Contractor?

Certainly, if your project is extensive, we don't recommend that you act as your own general contractor, but we know why you'd ask—it's easy to take one look at the mark-up for profit and overhead paid to general contractors (which typically runs between 15 and 20 percent of construction costs) and wonder why you should pay that to a general contractor instead of spending it on something else! You may be asking yourself "Isn't this something I can do?"

Acting as your own general contractor can be a recipe for disaster unless you really know what you're doing. So before you don your hardhat and strap on a tool belt, please think again. It will almost certainly cost you more than you would have paid the contractor—not only in cash but also in aggravation. You probably don't have the experience or the time to shop different trades to get the best deal. You may not understand how things proceed well enough to anticipate problems or keep your remodel on budget or schedule. You probably don't know how each system works and what specialists are needed to deal with many issues; you almost certainly will not know how the different tradesmen work together. You might even find that you will have to hire a general contractor after all to fix your mistakes. Being your own general contractor is also incredibly time-consuming. So, if you have a job or kids and find that you can't even fit in a weekly manicure or badly needed hair appointment, you most certainly don't have the time for this!

Does Every Job Require a General Contractor?

If your project is limited to one or two tasks, you might be fine without a general contractor. Some projects can be handled by a specific tradesman or even by a store that provides both materials and installation. For example, if you are simply repainting some rooms and installing new light fixtures, then you might just need to hire a painter and an electrician. But if you are doing a number of projects at the same time or there is any work that will be done that involves ripping through walls or affecting the home's systems, then you should give serious thought to hiring a general contractor rather than coordinating a bunch of specialists yourself.

When you don't hire a general contractor, you will still want to interview your tradesman, see his prior work, and get a bid, just like you would on a larger job. And be sure that your tradesman has a license and the proper insurance.

You should know that what you think is a small project may, however, entail much more than you think. Take the remodel of a small kitchen, for example. Who will do demolition and remove the old flooring? Who will remove all the appliances? If you move things around, who will repair holes in the walls? In what order do you schedule everyone from flooring people and the tile man to cabinet installers and painters? Who will clean up the mess? You might be better off hiring a general contractor to coordinate all these different trades.

WHY DO CONTRACTORS GET SUCH A BAD RAP?

Most general contractors have honest intentions, but that doesn't mean they are good or competent. Unfortunately, incompetent general contractors are not rare. Your whole project could be derailed if the contractor . . .

- **Underestimates you.** If the contractor is not good at estimating how much the job will cost, he may end up either cutting corners or charging more than he said he would.

- **Can't get his act together.** If the contractor is disorganized, he cannot coordinate schedules, which leads to delays and even problems with the work itself.

- **Two-times you.** If he has multiple jobs going at the same time but not a big enough operation or enough experience to run them all properly, expect problems. If a contractor doesn't have the manpower to handle multiple projects, he will often pull subs off one job in favor of another. Even if the quality of the work is not compromised, this can lead to delays.

- **Isn't experienced enough**. He might call himself a general contractor and he might think he can handle a large job just because he has some experience on smaller projects. Yet when he takes on a larger project, he really doesn't know what he's doing and he messes things up.

- **Doesn't work well with others**. If the contractor is not capable of working effectively with the rest of the team or managing his subcontractors on a day-to-day basis, the results are miscommunication and low morale. Subcontractors may then get lazy and do shoddy work, and the other professionals involved may get resentful.

- **Wheels and deals**. The contractor who is irresponsible or careless in financial matters and is always behind in paying his bills has the potential to cause serious problems: He might be taking money from one job to pay subs and material suppliers on another, leaving the first client's bills unpaid. In any case, money problems don't just mean late payments to subs and inability to purchase materials, they can also lead to the demise of the contractor's entire business. And you want your contractor to be around for a long time . . . you want him to be there to fix any problems even after your job is complete.

HOW TO AVOID BEING TAKEN ADVANTAGE OF

A woman needs to be careful about the kind of man she brings home. When looking for a contractor, make sure you do your research and get references. Otherwise, you may end up hiring a take-the-money-and-run type or someone who rips you off or does poor-quality work. Here are a few situations that should give you pause as you begin the search for a contractor.

Beware of Unsolicited Offers from Strangers

Beware of people who approach you at home improvement warehouses or paint stores, asking if you need to have any work done to your home. Likewise, if you are home during the day, you may have strangers ringing your doorbell or calling you on the phone offering the same thing. The person may have spotted the obvious flaw (your deteriorated driveway or peeling paint job) or offer you a service that you may or may not need. And you should know that these types of workmen more often prey on women than they do on men. You never know what you are getting yourself into when you don't know the contractor well enough. Consider Sheri's painting fiasco.

> Sheri had been thinking of hiring someone to repaint the outside of her house for quite some time, but she never seemed to get around to it between running her home business and driving the kids' carpool. So when Victor knocked on her door offering to do the job for what seemed like a reasonable price, she hired him without seeing any prior work or getting a single recommendation. Victor finished quickly, much to Sheri's delight, but she knew she had made a mistake when the paint started peeling almost immediately. Although Sheri's husband tried not to make her feel worse than she already did, he would not get off her case about the whole thing until she hired a reputable painter—after checking his references and seeing his prior work, of course. Sheri realized why Victor was finished so quickly—he had failed to do the proper sanding, priming, and other prep work her competent new painter was now doing . . . all for the same money she had paid Victor. She ended up paying twice, but at least she learned what not to do for any future renovations.

Beware of One-Time Offers

One-time deals are most likely pressure tactics. Never agree to hire someone who demands or pressures you to make a decision right then and there.

Beware of Deals That Seem Too Good to Be True

If a contractor's price is far below any other bid or estimate you have received, you should proceed with caution. The contractor may be desperate for work and may cut corners to be able to do your job for a low price.

DOES SIZE MATTER?
A Larger Contracting Business Versus a Smaller Operation

General contractors and their businesses come in different size packages. Bigger is not always better! The scope of your project will dictate which size is right for you.

Large Companies

Larger contracting businesses are like any large business—they have the capacity to take on bigger and more complex projects and usually have a number of jobs going on at a time. They may also employ or be affiliated with other professionals, such as structural engineers, architects, and designers. Large companies often handle the building or rebuilding of an entire home or a very significant remodel. So, if your project is a small one, this size company may not want to bid on the job at all or will not give the project priority when it has so many other larger, more lucrative ones. In fact, one of the first things you should discuss with any company is the scope of the work contemplated so you can weed out contractors who are not interested in your job. The advantage to hiring a large company is that it probably has a

> ### Meeting the Man You Are Going to Live With
>
> In a larger operation, there are often employees who handle the initial contact or first meeting with the company. That person may not perform any work on your job and may simply be a salesperson for the company. You should always make sure you meet the contractor and/or construction manager who will be assigned to handle your project before you hire the company since he's the one you'll be dealing with on a day-to-day basis.

number of crews, each dedicated to its own project—with some workers to spare on one job when another is done. With a dedicated crew assigned to your project, things usually get done more quickly.

Medium-Size and Small Companies

A medium-size general contractor usually employs regular subcontractors and handles several projects at the same time, and the owner tends to be very hands-on, spending a significant amount of time supervising jobs. Similarly, the owner of a small operation does a lot of the work himself with a few other workers, along with some regular subcontractors. The differences between the two are in the size and number of the projects handled and the number of employees or subs the contractor uses at once. If you are planning a major remodel but are not building an entire home, a medium-size operation may be best for you. A very small operation is most likely suited to handle only small projects that do not require a crew of workers. If your project is a smaller one and you hire a contractor who will be doing all the work himself, make sure he has all the necessary skills and qualifications to handle the work.

Design/Build Firms

A contracting company that also employs or is affiliated with architects and designers is called a design/build firm because it can handle the design as well as the construction of the project. A design/build firm could be a small or larger operation. As is the case with architects, design/build firms often specialize in a particular style of home or type of remodel (such as kitchen remodel). If you decide to go with a design/build firm, make sure the design you have in mind is in sync with the company's portfolio.

What Size Won't Tell You

Size does not necessarily translate into quality. It is important that you find out if your contractor has experience on a job like yours and that you actually see the work for yourself.

STARTING YOUR SEARCH FOR THE ONE

Once you decide to go forward with your project, you should immediately start your search, but don't rush the selection process even if you feel like you're in a hurry. We recommend interviewing a number of different contractors so that you have a basis for comparison. So set a lot of dates and don't settle for the first one. After all, breaking up is hard to do! Getting a divorce from your contractor and finding someone new will bring your project to a screeching halt. If you are careful at the outset and do not make a hasty decision, you will, by the end, save yourself time and money and spare yourself a lot of stress.

> ### Get On It
>
> Once you have made the decision to remodel, the more lead time you have the better. With many people remodeling these days, you may find that contractors in your area are booked solid.

SOURCES OF FIX-UPS:
Meeting Contractors

As is the case with romance, some sources of introductions are more reliable than others. Here's what you need to know.

- **People you know: relatives, friends, and neighbors.** When getting a referral from someone you know, you have the chance to see the contractor's work, ask a lot of questions, and (you hope) get truthful answers. But there can be a downside to hiring a friend or relative of your friend: Your friend could be making the recommendation based on the relationship, not based on confidence in or familiarity with the contractor's work.

- **People who know everyone: real estate brokers.** Good real estate brokers and agents will often keep track of contractors who have done the best jobs for their clients. Plus, a good broker has an incentive to give a good referral—it reflects well on the broker, just as a bad referral can reflect badly on the broker.

- **The insiders: subcontractors and other tradesmen.** Many good plumbers, electricians, painters, or other tradesmen know one or more qualified contractors in your area. So if you liked that guy who fixed your broken pipes under your house, find out who he recommends. Ask about his personal experiences with the contractor, including the quality of the contractor's work, job-site morale, and if he was paid on time. See if you can get him to talk about any problems that came up.

- **The professionals: architects and designers.** As is the case with real estate brokers and subcontractors, architects and designers often work with contractors on a regular basis and have a lot of information about them. The upside of hiring someone with whom your architect or designer has worked before is that they will be familiar with each other's work and style. The downside is that, since contractors and design professionals often refer clients to each other, this might not be the most objective recommendation. On the other hand, no reputable architect or designer will want to tarnish his or her own reputation with a bad referral.

- **The ads: the Internet, and other media**. Sure, an ad with great graphics or a stylish website can look impressive. But just because someone has spent the money to take out a lot of ad space or has hired a good Web designer doesn't mean he is qualified for the

job. A personal referral is always best, but if you find yourself hiring from an advertisement, you must scrutinize the person or company that much more carefully and, as always, get independent references. Nevertheless, there are some Internet sites that can be good starting points.

- **The clubs: business and trade organizations**. Local business bureaus, other business organizations, and certain local trade associations can often provide you with a list of contractor referrals in your area. Not every association tracks its members' conduct very carefully, so you'll still need to do your own homework.

THE MAYBES AND THE DEFINITELY NOTS:
Narrowing Down the List

Now it's time to set up a few dates. Ideally you should interview three to five candidates in person, and you don't want to waste your time interviewing someone who on the phone doesn't seem interested or is clearly not a match for you. So, as you make calls, tell the contractor about your project and listen for signs of initial interest. Ask certain preliminary questions. Cross off the names of contractors who don't give you the right answers on the phone or

There's No Place Like Home

*Y*ou may meet with a larger firm at its offices, but nothing can replace a meeting at your home so that the contractor can see the job site firsthand. So make sure, if you have your first meeting in an office, that you have another meeting at your home before you hire the contractor.

who don't sound professional. You'll find that the list of questions to ask yourself about a general contractor is surprisingly similar to those you would ask yourself about a potential love interest.

Prescreening Checklist

- **How does he look on paper?** Does the general contractor carry the proper license? (*Remember:* If your state requires one but he hasn't got it, then don't bother to set up a meeting!) Also, find out if he has any skeletons in his closet in the form of a lawsuit or complaint registered or filed against him, and whether it has been resolved or is still pending (see Resources). Keep in mind that, while a complaint filed against a contractor could be a huge red flag, it does not necessarily mean that your contractor did anything wrong. That's because anyone can file a complaint against anyone, whether the claim is legitimate or not. So if you really like this contractor, ask him about the situation when you meet him and see what he says.

- **Does he carry protection?** Does the general contractor carry general liability and workers' compensation insurance?

- **Can he handle you?** Does the general contractor think he can handle your type of project?

- **Can he commit to your time frame?** Is the general contractor available to start and complete the work when you need him to?

- **How old is he?** You might want to avoid a general contractor who has been in business for fewer than five years. He may not have enough experience and, according to the Better Business Bureau, a large percentage of contractors go out of business within the first five years due to incompetence or financial insolvency.

THE FIRST DATE:
Meeting and Interviewing Contractors

Because interviewing contractors is time-consuming, it may be tempting to allow yourself to fall for the first one you meet. But it is important to meet other people so you have a basis for comparison before you settle on the one. Also, the investment of time will be worth it; you may even get some good ideas from contractors you don't end up hiring—design-wise or otherwise—that you, a designer, or an architect hadn't thought of.

Drawing the Line in This Relationship

Striking a balance between a friendly yet businesslike relationship with a contractor often becomes a challenge as you get to know each other better and see each other frequently. If you can maintain this balance, you will have a much easier time dealing with problems as they arise.

Interview Etiquette

You will have plenty of time to use your feminine wiles to butter up your contractor *after* you hire him should the need arise. But right now, you will need to get down to business.

- **Make him respect you.** In a nice way, take charge of the meeting. Don't let him spend the entire meeting selling you on how great he is. Let him sell you by answering your questions so you will know how he compares to other contractors. Also, asking the right questions sends the first signal to the contractor that you are a woman who knows what she wants and is in charge!

One Big Happy Family

*I*f you have already started working with a designer or architect that you like and trust, it's a good idea to have that person meet the contractor of your choice before you commit to hiring him. And you will also want to introduce your contractor to all the critical people in your household such as your spouse or significant other, even if you think you will be the one primarily overseeing the contractor. Remodeling dramas of epic proportions often arise because members of the team or family don't get along with the contractor.

● **Don't be too pushy or neurotic.** A good contractor in a busy market may be choosy himself. He will also be sizing you up—he wants to determine whether he is interested in the project *and in working with you.* While you want to make sure you get answers to your questions, try not to seem overly anxious. And one more thing: Don't get too chatty. After all, you are hiring him to do a job for you and not to shoot the breeze or be your friend.

Your First Meeting

The more you open up to him, the better he'll know you, and the better he can satisfy your remodeling needs. That's why there are certain things that you should always communicate to a contractor in your first meeting, such as:

● How long you have owned the home.

● Whether you plan on living in the home during the remodel.

● Who you are working with already. For example, if you have already started working with an architect or designer.

● Where you are in the planning stage. Be sure to show him any plans, specs, or drawings that you have.

- Any special features, problems, or concerns about the project.

- Budgetary considerations. Sharing your budget and financial limitations with a contractor in the first meeting may give you a much-needed reality check. For example, you might want to change every aspect of your kitchen and think you can do it for $15,000, yet several contractors are telling you that your number is completely unrealistic. Now you know that you'll either have to rethink your plans or increase your budget *before* you have any contractor submit a bid. Otherwise, it is a waste of time for both of you.

Questions, Questions, and More Questions

You won't offend a reputable contractor with questions. In fact, he should expect you to ask a lot of them. If he clams up and is not responsive, it could be an indication that he doesn't have the answers or cannot communicate the way you need him to. Either way, he is probably the wrong guy for you! Here is a list of questions—some quite specific, and others a bit open-ended—that you will want to ask each candidate.

- **What type of work are you licensed to do?** Remember to get copies of all licenses and license numbers so you can check him out.

A Home Is Not an Office

Don't hire a contractor who has done mostly commercial work as opposed to residential. Renovating a home carries completely different considerations—from building codes to design considerations—and you want to make sure you hire someone with a good deal of experience in residential renovation.

- **What types of projects have you handled in the past?** Many contractors will naturally boast about the bigger projects they have handled in an effort to impress you, which is why you need to also ask the next question.

- **What types of projects do you typically handle or specialize in?** The answer to this question will give you more information about the contractor's typical project. It is important that he has a good deal of experience handling projects like yours. For example, a contractor who has handled many modest renovations such as bathroom overhauls is probably not the right person to take on the building of a whole new wing to a home if he's handled this type of project only once or twice.

- **How many projects do you handle at the same time?** If he's too busy, that could be a problem, and you'll need to ask if he has the time to handle your project.

- **How long have you been in business?** Again, we caution you against hiring someone who has been in business fewer than five years.

- **Do you work with a regular crew of subcontractors?** A contractor can most effectively manage his subcontractors when he has an established relationship with them and there is mutual trust and respect. This means that his jobs will be his subs' priority, and your contractor will have some leverage with the subs to correct any problems promptly. He will also be more familiar with the quality of their work if he regularly employs them. One thing to keep mind, however, is that if a contractor has an established crew he works with, he is less likely to get competitive bids on your project from other subcontractors. (For this reason, ideally, the contractor should have relationships with several different subs for each trade.)

- **Do you have an office or office manager?** A good general contractor must not only be able to do a good job of the physical work but must also be able to deal with the requisite paperwork. (He probably didn't become a contractor because he likes pushing paper, but if he is smart, he has someone in his back office keeping track of the paperwork if he's not good at it.) He must be able to prepare bids, prepare the contract, effectively schedule contractors, and be set up to pay them in a timely fashion. Many small- and medium-size contractors have an office set up in their home, and that is fine—there is no reason why you should have to go to his office. The important thing in an interview is to get a sense that the contractor is sufficiently well organized to be able to handle the clerical aspects of his job.

- **How much time will you be spending at my home supervising the project?** It's important that your contractor (or a supervisor in his employ that you and he trust) is present at all critical times during the project. Smaller contractors who do much of the work themselves may be there all the time, whereas contractors who have multiple projects going on at the same time may just stop by on a regular basis to make sure everything is proceeding the way it should be. It is important to get a handle on how the contractor works on a day-to-day basis and on how he supervises his subcontractors.

- **How would you handle *this* problem?** You may be aware of a particular challenge or problem with your project—now is the time to bring it up to the contractor. For example, you know that you have uneven flooring where you will be installing cabinetry or that you have had repeated leaks in a particular area of your home. Anything that you can think of that could be a potential problem should be brought to the contractor's attention so that you can get some insight into his problem-solving skills as well as his ideas on how to solve the particular problem.

- **How often do you clean up?** You must face the fact that your home will be a mess while all this work is going on. Still, some contractors are less sensitive to this. Dust and dirt from a variety of sources will most likely overwhelm the home as work is in progress. Talking about this is most critical if you are going to be living in your home during the remodel. Discuss with the contractor how he plans to protect your things—and your lungs—from dust and grime.

- **Will you be in charge of getting all the necessary permits, and arranging for inspections and sign-offs?** Remember, a general contractor should be knowledgeable about building codes to help you assess what you can and can't do, get the necessary permits, and arrange for any inspections that need to be done by your local building department.

- **Will you provide a written contract?** We have already alerted you to the importance of having a written contract with your contractor (see also Chapter 9). Any reputable contractor should be very professional about this one—he knows it's as important to him as it is to you to have a written contract. If he resists having a written agreement, then consider this as a huge warning sign—enough to have you cross him off your list of potential candidates.

- **Do you carry liability insurance and workers' compensation insurance; if so, how much are your policy limits?** Your contractor must have both types of insurance.

- **Do you have any questions?** It is important to give the contractor an opportunity to ask you any questions that he may have about your project.

- **Could I have several names and numbers of client references?** Try to get at least two references—a completed home and one under construction would be ideal. Look for projects that are similar to yours. Be sure to tell the contractor that you want to speak to his clients and see their homes.

The First Date Is No Time to Make a Commitment

At the first meeting, some contractors may try to pressure you to make a decision about hiring them. They may give you a rough estimate of costs, depending on the project's scope and complexity, and ask you to sign a document acknowledging the estimate. Do not sign anything! Remember, an estimate is not the same thing as a bid. As we said earlier, an estimate given during the first meeting is at best only very rough. Signing it, though, may be interpreted as a contract between you and the contractor for him to do the work at that price.

Taking Some Time to Think It Over

After you have met your candidates, take some time to think about the ones that are left on the list. Who impressed you most and why? With whom did you have the best rapport? It's no different with your contractor than with any other relationship. If you cannot communicate well with each other, things may get very tense during your remodel. You want a contractor who will explain what's going on as the project progresses, who will be able to discuss problems that arise, and who will work with you toward a great result. You also want to hire a contractor who is willing to help you refine or develop your plans in a cost-effective way.

No Show, No Go

One of the biggest complaints you hear about contractors is that they don't keep appointments or show up ridiculously late for meetings. If a contractor stands you up or is more than thirty minutes late, then do *not* give him a second chance. This is a sign of bad things to come. Remember, people are usually on their best behavior early on in a relationship. It rarely gets any better—it probably will only get worse. (It's one thing if he calls you ahead of time and needs to change the time of the meeting with good reason, but think twice if this call comes at the last minute.)

Warning Signs

On a date, you don't always know if a man is a definite yes for a relationship—sometimes it takes a few dates. But often you can tell a definite no right off the bat. A contractor is a definite no if he has any of these qualities:

- He doesn't have a required license.
- He doesn't have the proper insurance.
- He is intimidating, condescending, impatient, disrespectful, or makes you feel uneasy in any way.
- He seems uncomfortable about giving you names of previous clients, or refuses to do it at all.
- He puts pressure on you to hire him right away or asks you to sign something at the first meeting.
- He doesn't show up for the first meeting.

GETTING TO KNOW HIS PAST RELATIONSHIPS:
Checking References

After interviewing several contractors, you have a lot more information and are probably leaning in favor of one over the others. But your work is not done yet. It is time for you to check references.

A contractor should have no problem giving you names of previous and current clients. A good general contractor should be proud of his work and expect that you will want to check references. Not only will you want to speak to his former clients but you will want to go to their homes and see the work for yourself. Don't be shy about asking if you can see someone's home. Most homeowners are proud to show just about anyone their newly remodeled home and discuss the gory details . . . people love talking about their remodels!

Probably the most reliable references will come from someone you know who has used the contractor before. References provided by the contractor won't be quite as objective. Of course, the contractor will refer you to previous clients who will say nice things about him and will try to keep you away from anyone who has anything negative to say. Still, with good questions, a woman can get a lot of very valuable information.

When you get references from the contractor, it is a good idea to get the name of one client who has a job in progress and one client (or two, if possible) whose remodels are completed.

Do You Click?

*J*ust because he's right for someone else doesn't mean the two of you will click; whether you see any warning signs or just get that feeling that he might not work out for you, follow your instincts.

From these references you can get the following information:

State of the Remodel	What You Can Learn About the Contractor
Remodel in progress	Organization at the job site
	Current craftsmanship
	Relationship with subcontractors
Completed remodel	Soup to nuts: how the job progressed
	Ability to meet time and budget constraints
	How the project looks
	Follow-up after completion
	Correction of problems once the job was done

Doing Some Digging: What to Look for and What to Ask

Here's a list of what to look for when you walk through a home in which the work is completed:

- **Walls**. The surface should look seamless and not appear wavy or dimply.

- **Paint**. The coating should look even, the lines should be sharp where wall and ceilings and floors meet and where wall meets molding, paint on moldings should look neat and even.

- **Carpentry (moldings, built-ins)**. Lines should be clean and even, cuts where one piece of molding meets the next should look clean and neat. Molding should not have gaps between it and the surface to which it is attached. Cabinets should be screwed into the walls—not nailed in.

- **Flooring**. Look for level surfaces and even patterns, borders, and spacing (if applicable). For hardwood flooring, look at the quality of the staining or finishing.

- **Other details**. Make sure electric plates, knobs, and handles look like they are installed properly, that fixtures look evenly placed

---

Dollars and Delays

As we say over and over again, remodels often don't get finished on time and often go over budget. Remember, as often as not, owners are responsible for many delays, usually because they cannot make timely decisions or because they make changes in the middle of the project. But delays can also be the contractor's fault as well. So if a former client of the contractor's says the job was not finished in time or within the budget, find out why.

This is also the time to do a lot of prying. To find out how the client's experience was, it is essential that you have a discussion without the contractor being there. So if the contractor is there when you meet, make friends with the owner and call her later. Here is a list of questions to ask:

- What was the nature of your remodel? Which rooms were done and what type of work was done?
- Did the work start on time? Finish on time? Stay on schedule? If not, why?
- Was the project finished within the budget and, if not, why?
- Did everything go as planned? Were there any changes that needed to be made and, if so, why?
- Did you like the contractor?
- Did you like the contractor's subcontractors?
- Was the contractor organized?
- Did workers show up on time? Were they working all day?
- How often was the contractor (or his supervisor) at the work site?
- Did you feel that there was proper supervision of the subcontractors?
- Was there anyone else other than the general contractor acting in a supervisory role?
- Did you have any items stored at the job site and were those items well taken care of?
- Was the job site well secured?
- Was cleanup done on a regular basis? How often?
- Did you find the contractor to be reachable and accessible when you needed to talk to him?
- Was the contractor good at answering questions and explaining the process?
- Did you feel comfortable discussing any problems or concerns?
- Did you make any changes in the plans as you went along? If so, how did that go?
- Were you satisfied with the work?
- Was the contractor good about finishing punch list items?

- How is the work holding up?
- Were there any problems after the job was completed?
- Would you work with this person again?

For Love or for Money?

You are getting close to picking the one with whom you will be spending the rest of your life . . . uh, your renovation. You know that no matter how you feel about any one contractor or how good his reputation is, the final decision will also be about money. This doesn't just mean the cheapest bid—it means value and quality for your money, too. So before you make your final decision, you'll need to get bids from your remaining candidates to find out which of these contractors is willing to make a commitment you can live with. The next chapter will guide you through the bidding process.

8

His Proposal:
REVIEWING THE BIDS

Now that you have done some planning and talked with general contractors, you may have some cost estimates. But estimates are just that and give you only an idea of your budget. Merely having an idea, however, is not going to cut it. For you to take the next step, you will want to get several bids from several different contractors. If you have already started working with an architect or designer, he or she may assist you with this process as part of his or her services. Some architects and designers are better at sizing up bids than others. If you don't have an architect or designer, then you will have to obtain the bids yourself.

As you move forward, you should be aware of the difference between bids and cost estimates. A bid is a commitment, but an estimate is just talk. As we have already stressed, *even if it is in writing,* an estimate is just a rough approximation of what the contractor thinks your job will cost. It doesn't mean he's committing to do your project for that price. By contrast, a bid (once signed by the contractor) is a proposal from him to do the work for the cost

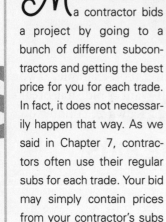

stated in the bid if you hire him. So, let's say a contractor gives you an *estimate* that your project will cost $100,000, and based on this, you move forward with him and have him start work without getting a formal bid. In the end, you could easily be hit with bills totaling twice that. By contrast, if you had gotten a *bid* for a hundred thousand, you wouldn't be in this predicament.

Just like with estimates, to come up with a bid, a contractor will need as much information and detail as you and anyone else involved (such as your architect, designer or structural engineer) can give him. A complete set of plans is ideal, but give your contractor anything else that will help him get a handle on what you want to do, such as a photograph of someone else's remodel, a sketch or a picture from a magazine. When the subject of bids comes up, make sure you tell the contractor that you want as much detail as possible and that you are not just after the bottom line.

THE ANATOMY OF A BID

A bid should break down, in detail, line by line, the cost of each aspect of the project. If the contractor has enough information about the project, ideally he should organize his bid logically, in the chronological order of the different stages of the project (for example, demolition first, followed by framing). For each stage, the bid should describe the cost of labor and materials for each trade (for example, electrical or plumbing) and should also include any supervisory fees, administrative costs, allowances and contingencies, and the contractor's percentage markup for profit and overhead, as explained later.

Elements of the Job

The section of the bid containing the elements of the job consists of line items for all costs associated with the project supplied by the contractor, including labor and materials (whether supplied by the contractor or a subcontractor or tradesman), equipment, appliances, hardware, fixtures, and all other items necessary for the job. A well-prepared bid should be very specific. For example, if you are remodeling an entire kitchen, you will want a bid that breaks down the cost for the flooring, cabinetry, hardware, countertops, backsplash, wall finishes, each appliance (assuming the contractor will be responsible for ordering and installation), each fixture, electrical work (wiring, switch plates, electrical outlets), lighting, ventilation work, and any window work (if applicable). It should also detail brand, style, finish, color, model number, and so on; or if you have not determined all of these things, there should be a place in the bid to fill these things in and an allowance or contingency for them. (Allowances and contingencies are explained later.)

Other Costs Listed in the Bid

- **Reimbursable and administrative costs**. A contractor might want to be reimbursed for certain costs, like travel, parking, phone, and photocopying.

- **Supervision**. If your project is a big one, your contractor may recommend, or you may want to have, a construction supervisor on a regular basis for all or part of the job. A construction supervisor is someone who will spend a significant amount of time at the job site supervising the subcontractors and reporting back to you, the contractor, and your architect or designer (if you have one). If your contractor provides these services, he will usually charge a separate fee.

- **Allowances and contingencies**. Yes, we've told you that this is the time to get your contractor to commit to all the costs of the project, yet the truth is that, even if you have detailed plans, there are still unknowns. Allowances account for the things you haven't chosen yet—for example, maybe you haven't picked out your bathroom tile or hardware, so the contractor builds in an estimated budget or a budget range for these things in the bid. The contingency is an amount built into the bid to cover the unexpected.

Contractor's Profit and Overhead

The contractor could charge anywhere from 10 to 25 percent or more of the total job for his profit and overhead (his fee). Most contractors charge in the 15 to 20 percent range—10 percent is low for the industry; 25 percent is considered high, but there are contractors out there who charge this amount or even more. Keep in mind that just because he asks you to pay for something doesn't mean you have to agree to it. Charges that you can often negotiate down or out altogether are markups on reimbursable and administrative costs, such as overhead he is trying to pass on to you (like the cost to keep his office running).

THE BOTTOM LINE:
Fixed-Price Versus Cost-Plus Arrangements

It is easier with some remodeling projects than with others to determine at the outset what a job will cost. Conventional wisdom would dictate that you get the contractor to commit to a set price for your project whenever possible because then you'll know exactly what you are getting yourself into. However, there may be several reasons why this may not be possible. Perhaps you have an older home, and the contractor feels that there are too many unknowns to be able to quote you a fixed price. (For example, he may be worried about what he will find inside the walls.) Next we explain the different ways to establish a price for your remodel and whether or not it is realistic to know what the total cost will be at the outset.

Fixed Price

A fixed-price bid sets a total price for the job that the contractor commits to. For example, $100,000 to remodel a kitchen, bathroom, and laundry room. For a smaller project, it might be possible for a contractor to determine a fixed price without detailed plans, but for a larger job the contractor will probably need you to provide extensive plans and specs.

Cost-Plus

If it will be difficult to determine at the outset how much the different

Are You Serious About Him?

As you can imagine, preparing a formal bid is time-consuming for a contractor, and he may not want to prepare one unless he thinks he has a real shot at being hired. So don't lead him on! If you don't think you want to work with him, don't ask him to prepare a bid. But if you think he might be the one, let him know you're interested, and that you'd like to get a bid.

ent elements of the job will cost, either because you haven't settled on firm plans or because there are too many unknowns about your home, then it may be that you enter into a cost-plus arrangement with your contractor. Here, you pay the contractor the actual cost for labor, materials, equipment, plus a markup for his overhead and profit. You and your contractor establish these costs as the remodel goes along. So, unlike a fixed-price arrangement, with a cost-plus contract, you don't know exactly what your project will cost before your contractor starts work.

Remodeling a fixer home is the classic situation that calls for a cost-plus arrangement. The contractor finds it too difficult to come up with a fixed price at the outset because he knows that there is a lot he won't know about the home until after he can open up the walls. Sometimes people also enter into cost-plus arrangements when they are eager to start remodeling but haven't yet settled on firm plans. This can happen for a variety of reasons. Regardless of the circumstances, it is the remodeler who enters into a cost-plus arrangement who often gets into trouble with costs spiraling out of control.

Even with a cost-plus arrangement, there may be many costs that your contractor can commit to right from the start. For example, you may be refinishing your existing wood floors, and this cost can usually be determined right away. Get as many bids as you can for different elements of the job as soon as possible.

Pin Him Down

Even in a cost-plus arrangement, don't let a contractor start any work unless you have agreed to the cost in avance. Just because you're figuring it out as you go doesn't mean you don't get bids. You should always get bids for every aspect of the job as soon as the price can be determined—you just won't be able to determine the cost of every element of the job before your project starts. So, for example, your contractor might not be able to get a comprehensive bid for electrical work at the outset of the job because he doesn't yet know the state of the wires in the walls, but he can still obtain a bid for an exterior paint job. And don't let him start the electrical work until he can tell you what it will cost.

Which Arrangement?

When careful planning has been done and the contractor has been given very specfic information about what the client wants, and when there are not too many unexpected surprises or unknowns about a home, a fixed-price bid is usually the ideal arrangement. There are certain issues you should be aware of. If there are many unknowns about the project, a fixed-price arrangement may not be the right way to go because the contractor may have inflated his bid greatly to protect himself against these unknowns. The risk to the contractor in a fixed-price arrangement is that it is possible that he has underestimated the cost of your job. If this turns out to be the case, then not only will he not make a profit but he may also have to pay for your project out of his own pocket. Now, you would think that a contractor who has underestimated the cost of your job has unknowingly given you a good deal and that this is a good thing. But, actually, this could be as bad news for you as it is for him. The contractor may very well find ways to cut corners in an effort to lose as little money as possible.

In a cost-plus arrangement, you don't have these potential problems, but there can be others. A cost-plus project can be a recipe for a runaway budget because it is so open ended. Problems can arise if you are not on top of your project, if you have an untrustworthy contractor (or simply one who is not mindful of the budget), or if you are constantly changing and adding things as you go. Cost-plus arrangements sometimes include a guaranteed maximum price so costs don't get way out of hand, but many contractors will not agree to this. To avoid the pitfalls of a cost-plus arrangement, read Chapter 9 very carefully!

Be aware of the fact that you may not have much of a choice between one type of arrangement or another. If there are too many unknowns about the project before work begins, a good contractor will tell you that he can't give you a fixed price for the job at the outset.

Time and Materials

A time-and-materials contract is a third type of financial arrangement you can make with a contractor, but it isn't always practical for larger jobs. Here, a contractor charges an hourly rate for his time (and the time spent by any employees), plus the cost of materials. It is fairly uncommon to do a major project on a time-and-materials basis; it would simply be too expensive and impractical. Time-and-materials contracts are more common on smaller projects or portions of projects, or when a single trade is involved. Think of a time-and-materials arrangement the way you would when you call a plumber because your shower won't drain. You know you have a plumbing problem, but you aren't sure what it might be or how much it might cost to fix. Your plumber charges you a set amount for a service call and then by the hour after that, plus materials, to diagnose the problem and fix it.

MEETING TO DISCUSS THE BIDS

Once a contractor has prepared his bid, he will probably want to meet with you. This is a good idea so that you can go over everything and ask any questions you have. Go into this meeting respecting that he has invested time in your project by preparing the bid, but be aware of the fact that he may try to pressure you into making a decision right then and there. For example, he may tell you that he is really busy and needs an answer right away because he is considering other projects that he will take if you don't hire him.

Do not succumb to pressure! Do not make your decision immediately after being handed the bid and, as we've said before, do not sign anything. You are not, at this point, committing to use a particular contractor. If you sign the bid, it could be interpreted to be a contract between the two of you. You must have time to review the bid yourself without the contractor there and you should compare it against other bids. You should also review it with your advisers and your significant other, and anyone else involved with the project. In any case, you will not want to sign anything until you have a fully negotiated contract, to which the bid should be attached.

ARE YOU AND YOUR CONTRACTOR ON THE SAME PAGE?
Making Sure the Bid Reflects the Remodel You Have in Mind

This is the time to make sure you and the contractor understand each other. As you review the bid from each contractor, you'll find out if he knows what you're thinking and if his bid accurately reflects the job you had in mind—from the type of flooring, paint, and finishes you want to use to the brand of fixtures and appliances you like. If any bid does not, then you will want to figure out why. It could be your fault—you may not have provided enough detail, although an experienced contractor should have pointed this out to you. Or it could be that the contractor doesn't know how to prepare a bid properly. If the problem lies with your failure to communicate, then you must give the contractor more detailed information. But if it's your contractor who just doesn't get it, then no matter how much you liked him, he's not the man for you—don't hire him!

COMPARING BIDS

Compare the bids you receive. You can use them to pick and choose your contractor. But don't just choose the cheapest bid while dismissing higher bids, especially if the higher bid came from the contractor you like best. Instead, you can use the lower bid as a way to negotiate an acceptable price with the contractor that you really have your heart set on using.

Look Carefully at Allowances

*I*f one contractor's bid is higher than another's, take a careful look at the allowances and contingencies. Some contractors will try to reduce their bids by being cheap with allowances—that is, they will underestimate the cost of certain things that have not yet been decided, such as the type of finishes they expect you will choose. A contractor with higher allowances might be more realistic about your taste and home, so don't necessarily be scared off by higher allowances.

Tracy and her husband, James, were planning an extensive renovation of their home: a kitchen remodel, plus adding a second story that would give them three additional bedrooms. Tracy knew this renovation was going to be a big part of her life for the next year or more, and she knew how important it was to have a general contractor that both she and her husband liked and trusted. After meeting with three general contractors and checking references, the couple felt that Greg was the contractor for them, but they went ahead and got bids from all three. After hearing from Greg's references how reasonable his prices were, Tracy and James were surprised that his bid for carpentry work and painting came in significantly higher than the other contractors, whereas the bids for all other aspects of the job looked competitive with the other contractors. When they spoke to Greg about it, he explained that his painters were a bit pricey because they were very sophisticated in doing specialty faux finishes. Greg also realized that the finish carpentry bid was higher because he had mistakenly priced the wrong materials; the bid reflected a price for a more expensive type of wood than intended for the project. Greg got a bid from less-expensive painters since Tracy didn't want specialty finishes, and he adjusted the price for the finish carpentry work using the correct materials. Tracy and James hired him for the job.

The moral of the story: Ask questions and comparison shop! Had they not, Tracy and James would not have known that some of Greg's prices were higher than they needed to be. They used the other bids to educate themselves and to negotiate a better deal with the contractor they wanted.

Bids That Are High, Low, and Somewhere in Between

You shouldn't worry too much about minor discrepancies among bids. But if one bid comes in much higher than the rest, you may not want to hire that contractor. And what about a bid that is much lower than the rest? Take a closer look because it might not be the bargain it seems like it is. Just like when you buy a pair of shoes: You don't necessarily need a pair of Manolo Blahnik's; but if you go for the cheapest ones, they may end up causing you a lot of pain and you'll have to throw them away! It's the same with contractors. So be a little suspicious of the cheapest one. A contractor may have given you a low bid because his business is

---

Is He Desperate?

Be on the lookout for the desperate contractor who gives you a great price because he needs the work. To do your project for the price he gave you, he may cut corners or use subcontractors who are subpar. Sometimes contractors will underbid a job just to get it, will not be able to cover the costs of that job, and will then underbid the next job because they need the flow of money to catch up with their bills. This is a vicious cycle that is unfortunately all too common . . . a contractor who falls into it can eventually go out of business because he never catches up and never can recover.

---

not going well and he is desperate for work. Or perhaps he doesn't know what he's doing and can't accurately bid out a job.

On the other hand, a bid that is significantly lower than the others could be good news. There may be very good reasons for a lower bid: The contractor might actually have some creative ways—or solid business practices—that will save you money. For example, for one woman's bathroom remodel, the contractor suggested installing a frosted-glass interior door instead of a skylight to illuminate a windowless area. This suggestion shaved a few thousand dollars off the bid and was a better solution than the owner, architect, or designer had been able to come up with!

In the end, the bid must be put in the context of the contractor's

Bids Can Make You Feel Bitchy

*I*f all the bids come in higher than you expected, you may feel stressed, frustrated, or even resentful as you realize that this project will cost you more than you had thought or that you can't do the work that you wanted to do. Don't get nasty with the contractor. This is the time to use your charm to negotiate a little. If he really wants the job, there are certain costs he may be able to trim down a bit. So take a deep breath and get into negotiation mode.

other fine (or not so fine) qualities. Look for a fair price and analyze the overall picture. Consider reputation and references, experience and price, as well as personality and business practices. Who did you like best? Factor in any differences in what the contractors are offering and the skills they bring to your project. Then consider his willingness to make suggestions and offer advice, and the likelihood of the contractor standing behind his work. You may be lucky enough to have a hard choice, but chances are you'll have a frontrunner. Choose the contractor you think offers the best overall package.

Getting Ready to Tie the Knot:
WHAT YOU NEED TO KNOW BEFORE YOU SIGN A CONSTRUCTION CONTRACT

AT LONG LAST: After meeting a lot of different men, you are ready to settle down with the contractor of your dreams. But wait: Before you two tie the knot, you must make sure you and he are in complete agreement about the commitment you are about to make to each other. You should make it official by negotiating and signing the right written contract *before* you hire him.

If you are like most people, you probably have little or no experience with construction contracts, and the notion of negotiating one is a daunting prospect. In fact, because many women feel intimidated by all the fine print or can't be bothered, they make the mistake of doing a deal on a handshake or just signing on the dotted line when a piece of paper is handed to them. Whether your project is big or small, don't make this mistake!

Without the *right* contract, you'll be vulnerable to all sorts of things that can go wrong on a remodeling project. Sure, on a handshake, your contractor might commit to a $75,000 budget and a six-month schedule, but you'll be one unhappy lady if the budget balloons to $150,000 and the completion date drags out another four or six months. Or what if a worker falls off a ladder and gets hurt? Or if a subcontractor smashes his car into your next-door neighbor's retaining wall? And how much money should you hand your contractor to get him started, and how do you protect yourself from his skipping town with the cash?

Fortunately, you can address all of these issues—and many more predicaments—if you get it in writing before a hammer hits a single nail. In this chapter, we discuss the provisions that every contract should have.

A TEST OF YOUR RELATIONSHIP

A good contract will protect you if something goes wrong or things don't work out. But that's not all. Negotiating the contract will give both of you the chance to discuss your expectations and obligations before you make a commitment. In fact, it will give you a preview of what it will be like to work together. After all, like the beginning of any relationship, your contractor will (or should be) on his best behavior while he's wooing you. He should be patient, understanding, and courteous. If you find that he's being impatient or unreasonable in the beginning, then chances are he'll be that way, or even worse, later on after he's already won you over! You might say that the time when you are trying to work out the terms of your contract is a little like living together before you get married. And, if a contractor resists signing a contract or tries to pressure you into signing something you haven't reviewed or don't feel comfortable with, that's a bad sign and you should back away from the whole thing!

WHO PREPARES IT AND WHAT IT LOOKS LIKE

Typically, a contractor will hand you his own contract, which he has prepared. If you are working with a lawyer, your lawyer may be happy to work with the contractor's form or will prepare her own form if she thinks the contractor's isn't quite up to snuff. Most contractors use preprinted forms; some forms are available in stationery stores. For larger jobs involving architects, contractors often use forms that are put out by the American Institute of Architects (AIA). These forms also refer to the architect's services and role in protecting you as the owner.

Some preprinted forms are better than others, and it's never easy to read a lot of small print. The form of a contract will vary from contractor to contractor and, of course, every job is different. It's essential that your contract be reviewed carefully. There may be provisions in the form that you want taken out and there will be, almost certainly, things you want to change and add. The next section walks you through key provisions.

Don't Worry About What He Thinks

Don't be tempted to sign whatever the contractor puts in front of you or to forgo all that legal stuff altogether just because you feel comfortable with this man or because you don't want to seem like you don't trust him. A reputable contractor shouldn't have a problem discussing the contract with you and should be ready for your questions and concerns. After all, the contract is for his benefit, too, and he will also want protection if something goes wrong—like if you don't pay him.

THE CONTRACT MUST-HAVES:
An Overview of the Necessary Provisions

The Date the Contract Takes Effect

The contract needs to be dated, and it needs to state when it takes effect. The effective date could even be a date before the signing of the contract. For example, if your contractor did some work before you signed the contract (this is a no-no, but it does happen), then the effective date may be the date that the work began. Also, it's important to have the contract reflect the date each of you signed it—you can write the date next to the signature.

Parties and Key-Man Provisions

The concept of the *parties* to your contract simply means who is entering into the contract: You (and your spouse or partner, if applicable), on the one hand, and the contractor, on the other hand. This seems like the most obvious of provisions, but there is a twist: If the contractor is a company (like a corporation, partnership, or some other entity), then you will be signing your contract with the entity. This means that the entity, and not any individual person, will be obligated to work on your project. But what about the person you have come to know and trust? Let's call him Bob. Bob works for a construction company that you are hiring. He's the one you interviewed, and he's the one you know best; in fact, he might be the only one you know. And he's the one who knows your project. You want to work with Bob, and you don't necessarily want to work with anyone else who works for this company. You can address this in the contract by asking for a *key-man* or *key-person* clause. This clause will state that a particular individual will be working on your project and that you have the right to terminate the contract if that person is no longer working for the company or involved with your project for any reason. You can make anyone—a construction supervisor or anyone else who works for the contractor—a key man or key person so long as the contractor agrees.

Sign-Off Power Is Key

*A*lthough you are much better off planning your remodel as much in advance as possible and going into it with detailed plans and specs to give to the contractor and to attach to the contract, the reality is that, for many people, remodeling is an evolving process. And things change as you go along. Make sure that the contract states that you must sign off on any new work, new plans, or changes to the plans after the contract is signed and before work begins.

Contact Information

List the name, physical address, phone number, fax number, and e-mail address for you, your contractor, and (if applicable) your construction supervisor.

Contractor's Credentials

Include the contractor's license number, if a license is required by your state (see Resources).

Description of Your Project

It is essential that the contract spells out with as much detail as possible the work to be done so that everyone's expectations are clear and so that you know that everyone is on the same page. This can be done several ways in the contract.

- **Short and sweet.** A simple description of the work in the contract is okay but *only* if you have detailed plans, specs, and bids that can be referred to and attached as part of the contract. Examples of simple descriptions are "Approximately 1,000-square-foot addition to home, including fourth bedroom, third three-quarter bath (shower/tub combined), closets, service porch, and small deck" and "Bathroom remodel, including new plumbing, replacement of existing fixtures and new tile."

- **No plans and specs.** If you do not have detailed plans and specs, you should make sure the description of the job in the contract is as specific as possible so that the contractor's obligations will be as clear as possible. Attach any drawings as an exhibit. If lengthy, the detailed description can also be done as an attachment to the contract.

Materials List

The contract should contain a detailed list of all appliances, fixtures, and materials to be used. Sometimes it's part of the bid (which you will attach to the contract) or sometimes it is a separate part of the contract (either in the body of the contract or as an attachment). The description should list all the items you are going to choose yourself, and should include, to the extent possible, brand names, colors, model numbers, and types of products. Some of these things may seem obvious to you; for example, which model refrigerator, washing machine, type of flooring or light fixtures you'll want. But you also have to think about the less obvious things such as what type of electrical plates, light switches, door knobs, and other hardware you want. If you do not specify what it is that you want, you'll be leaving it up to the contractor to choose and then you may have no control over what you'll get.

No Substitutions Please

Eliminate the words "or equivalent" in the contract next to any description of materials to be used. This is dangerous language and allows the contractor to make choices that you may not be happy with. Think about how important brands are . . . a woman who likes the fit of Levi's won't be happy with any other brand! Chances are you'll feel the same way about your refrigerator, dishwasher, toilet, sink, or even paint. And make sure your contract does not let your contractor make any substitutions without your written consent.

Materials Provided by the Contractor and Those Provided by You

As part of the materials list, you should spell out which items you will provide (for example, you may be buying all your own appliances and arranging for them to be delivered to the home) and which items your contractor will order on your behalf.

List of Subs

Ask that the contract include a list of subcontractors (painters, plumbers, electricians, etc.) who will be working on your project and include their addresses, phone numbers, and applicable license numbers and insurance certificates. We should note that contractors like to be in control of their subs and often guard the information that will allow you to contact the subs directly. If your contractor will not provide this information, the contract should let you disapprove of any subs you don't like.

Contract Price

In Chapter 8, we told you about different financial arrangements you can make with a contractor: fixed-price, cost-plus, and time-and-materials. A fixed-price contract should state the total cost of the job. A cost-plus or time-and-materials agreement should spell out what you are paying the contractor for (for example, labor, materials, overhead, and profit).

Payment Schedule

Contractors are typically paid in installments (often called *progress payments*). The most important thing about the payment schedule is that you want to keep your contractor on his toes as much as possible. In other words, you want your contractor to have as much incentive as possible to complete the work by making him wait for payment until the work is done . . . and done right! A typical payment schedule includes three stages.

Deposit

A contractor will often want a deposit before work starts, especially on a larger job, so that he can purchase materials to begin the work. The typical deposit usually runs between 5 and 10 percent. Keep in mind that the less you pay up front, the better off you are; you want to have the work stay ahead of the payments as much as possible, and not the other way around—otherwise, your contractor could take the money and run or use your money for other jobs instead of yours. Try to keep the deposit to a minimum. (Some states even regulate the maximum amount a contractor can ask for as an up-front payment.)

Too Much Too Soon?

*R*ather than giving your contractor the entire deposit on the signing of the contract, see if he'll agree to a smaller payment at that time with the balance to be paid on the date he starts the work.

Keep Him on a Tight Leash

*I*f you want to keep your project on a tight schedule and within budget, don't be easy with your progress payments. Instead, you should pay your contractor's invoice only after completion of the work described in the bill. If you are working with an architect or designer, he or she should be able to help you review the invoices.

Subsequent Payments

A typical contract will call for payments at regular intervals throughout the duration of the project. For a small project (such as the remodel of one bathroom), it is common for the owner to make an initial deposit followed by another substantial payment when work is about halfway done, with the final payment to be made when the work is finished.

For more extensive projects, progress payments are made more frequently. It is a good idea to tie progress payments to the different stages of completed work (see Chapter 14). So, for example, you will pay a percentage on completion of demolition, a percentage on completion of framing (rough carpentry), and a percentage on completion of the initial plumbing work (rough plumbing) and the initial electric work (rough electric work). On larger projects, some contractors will want to submit invoices for payment every few weeks for work done and materials delivered since the previous invoice, with payment due within a week or two.

Final Payment and Retainage

You should not make the final payment until every single aspect of the job is completed to your satisfaction. The work should be approved by your local building department and other necessary

Excuse Me, Sir, You're Not Quite Done!

There will be a point at which it feels to you as if your remodel is done. After all the planning, hard work, and stress, you are finally able to move in. Or, if you stayed in the home during the remodel, life finally seems to be getting back to normal. But there may be small things left to do. These are commonly known as *punch list items.* For example, knobs still need to be installed, paint needs to be touched up, or certain fixtures still need to be put in. One of the common complaints you hear about contractors is that it takes forever to get these punch list items taken care of. Why does this happen? Because many people make their final payment to the contractor before he finishes the punch list; and with all his subs having moved on to other projects, he has little incentive to complete these relatively minor things. So be smart: Withhold the final payment until your punch list items are completed as well.

Make Sure Everything Works

*I*n addition to making sure all the work is completed before you make your final payment, it is also a good idea to test everything out at least a few times before the contractor gets that final check. Forget about what season it is: If it's 95 degrees outside, you should light a fire in your new fireplace; if there's snow on the ground, you still need to try out that new air-conditioner.

governmental authorities (this usually involves final sign-off by the building department but may also involve sign-offs by local utility companies and other authorities as well). In addition, you should pay only if no mechanic's liens have been filed or can be filed (more on this later), and if the punch list has been completed.

The final payment should represent a substantial percentage of the job so that the contractor stays interested and has the incentive to finish up rather than moving on to another project. The larger the final payment, the better—ideally, the final payment should be 15 to 20 percent of the total contract price.

On a larger job, you can keep your contractor interested and give him added incentive to finish the job by negotiating a retainage (also known as a holdback) that is held from each progress payment (commonly 5 to 10 percent) and not paid until you make the final payment.

Payments to Subs and Suppliers, and Mechanic's Liens

There is always the possibility that a contractor will fail to pay his subcontractors. (This can be a problem because, in some states, even if a contractor is paid in full, the homeowner can still be liable for unpaid bills to subcontractors and suppliers). It is less likely that this will happen to you if you've been careful in choosing your contractor, but you do need to protect yourself against the possibility. If this happens, depending on your state's law, the sub or supplier could put a lien on your home (called a mechanic's lien) and sue you to have your home sold so that his claim can be paid. Although having your home sold is an extreme remedy and although it usually doesn't get to that point, having a mechanic's lien against your property can be a major inconvenience; it is hard to get a home loan or to sell your home with a mechanic's lien filed against it. But there are a few things you can do to protect yourself.

- **Waiver of mechanic's lien clause.** First, the contract should contain a clause requiring each sub and supplier to waive its right in writing to file a mechanic's lien each time the sub or supplier is paid on the job. The waiver is with respect to the particular payment received at the time. It may seem like a lot to keep track of during a job that has a lot of subs, but it's worth it.

- **Paying by two-party check.** Try to negotiate a clause in the contract that gives you the right to pay by two-party check (that is, a check made payable by you to both the contractor and the sub or supplier). Even better, ask for a clause that gives you the right to pay the subs and material suppliers directly. You still have the option of paying your contractor directly; but with a clause like this, you'll have the option of paying the subs instead if you think the contractor isn't paying or won't pay.

Permits and Approvals

The contract should state who is responsible for obtaining what. You will be responsible for obtaining approval of your plans from your homeowner's association if you live in a co-op, condo, or planned community (see Chapter 5). Your contractor should be responsible for obtaining any building permits, although you will typically be responsible for paying for any required permit fees (see Chapter 13).

Make Him Responsible

*I*t is critical that your contractor assume the responsibility for getting the permits. In most places, it is the person or business whose name is listed on the permit that is responsible if the work does not comply with the applicable local codes. One of the things you are paying your contractor for is to make sure that the work gets done in accordance with code. And if something needs to be corrected because it wasn't done to code, make sure it's your contractor who pays to fix it.

Commencement Date

The contract should spell out a date or the circumstances (such as getting plans approved) that trigger the contractor's obligation to start the work. Otherwise, he could start whenever he likes. Keep in mind, though, that just because the work starts by a certain date doesn't mean that things will necessarily stay on track. The contractor could make an appearance with his crew and then not come again for days or weeks. That's why it's so important to stay on top of things and make sure everyone is working, and why it's also important to have a completion date in your contract.

Keeping the Work on Schedule

Particularly for large jobs, it is common for the contract to contain a schedule with certain target dates (for example, completion of rough electrical and plumbing work, and installation of cabinetry) but it is not customary for the contract to spell out any remedy in the event any target date (other than the completion date) is not met. Throughout this book, we give you tips for keeping your project on schedule. In addition to having a completion date and perhaps an agreement that the contractor will pay you a certain amount for every day or week he is late completing the job, it is important to have weekly meetings to make sure the work is proceeding on schedule.

Keeping the Control and Meeting Regularly

*I*t would be ideal for your contract to contain a clause that allows you to inspect the work periodically and reject any work that doesn't meet with your approval. However, most contractors will resist this kind of a clause, and for good reason: It could give you too much latitude to disapprove of any work on a whim. (Of course, *you* know that you will be reasonable, but the contractor doesn't know that . . . yet.) But there's still a way to keep control and stay on top of things: Make sure your contract requires—and you attend—meetings with the contractor to discuss how things are progressing. Depending on the size and stage of the job, you might be meeting every week once construction gets going, and your architect or designer (if you have one) should be there, too. Also, you should show up at the job site as often as possible. The contract should require the contractor to build in accordance with any plans and bids, and the law will require him to build in accordance with industry standards and local codes; your attention and presence will help move things along in the right direction.

Completion Date

Your contractor may be the new man in your life but this is not a relationship that you want to last a lifetime! The contract should provide a date of completion—on a big job, a specific date for *substantial completion* (that is, completion of all work except for the punch list items). You will find that many contractors will not want to give you a firm completion date because the nature of renovations, especially certain types of renovations (such as in an older fixer home), is that you never know what you may find that will require additional work. It's all the things we've been warning you about throughout this book—unanticipated problems, weather delays, and so on. If a contractor is going to agree to a firm completion date, he may (and should) insist that he isn't responsible for delays beyond his control. If after discussion, he still won't agree to a firm completion date and you still want to use him because he has a good reputation and everything has checked out, suggest a date that is farther off in the future than the two of you had originally discussed as the target completion date. In other words, give him room for the unexpected. It's better than not having any completion date at all!

Liquidated Damages and Bonuses

When the contractor breaches the contract by not finishing by a completion date that is spelled out in the contract, he is legally responsible for money damages he's caused you if it is his fault. The exact amount of these damages is what people fight about in court.

You can save yourself the hassle and expense of fighting in court (and also give your contractor added incentive to finish your job on time) by figuring out your damages ahead of time and putting in the contract an amount that would compensate you for every day or week that your contractor is late finishing the job. These are called *liquidated damages*. Liquidated damages clauses are usually found in contracts for larger projects (contractors usually won't agree to this type of clause for a small project) and can be especially important if you are not living in the home during the renovation and therefore have double living expenses as a result. Every day that you cannot move in on time means paying at least another day's rent or more. You might have other expenses as well, such as boarding your pets. Take these expenses and estimate what it will cost you for each day or week that your contractor is late finishing the job. But also be prepared that your contractor may want something in return for giving you a liquidated damages clause—he may want a bonus for every day that he completes the work ahead of the stated completion date. This may seem fair, but keep in mind that too much incentive for early completion could lead to rushed or shoddy work. If you agree to a bonus, the amount does not need to be the same amount as the liquidated damages amount.

When It's Not His Fault

In all fairness, the contractor should not be responsible for missing the completion deadline if the delays are caused by you, governmental authorities, the architect or other team member, bad weather, unexpected or hidden conditions at the property that you discover during construction, or any cause besides the contractor. It's not unreasonable for the contractor to ask for this provision.

Use the Right Words

You can't put in extra costs to punish your contractor for being late—that would be a penalty and that's not allowed by law. So make sure the clause in your contract specifies your estimate of the damages you will suffer if he is late, such as estimates for storage or rent for every day you cannot move in. In most states, you'll need to make sure it is called a liquidated damages clause and not a penalty clause, or you won't be able to enforce it against your contractor.

Change Orders:
Changing Your Mind Is a Woman's Prerogative

It doesn't matter how much planning you've done in advance—chances are you'll still need or want to make changes to your project midstream. It could be that something unforeseen comes up that makes a change in plans inevitable, such as a change in your financial situation or a hidden problem with your home that emerges that requires additional work. Or maybe you've just changed your mind or want to add something. This is why one of the key provisions in the contract addresses changes or modifications to the agreed-on work after the contract is signed. The contract should provide that these changes, called *change orders*, be made in writing and signed by both you and the contractor. A change order is actually an amendment to the contract and should be done even for the smallest change. The change order should show the cost of the change—usually an increase in the cost of the job. The cost for the change should be bid by the contractor just as he bid out the initial work. When you sign the bid for the new work, make sure it includes the cost for the contractor's fee. Also, keep in mind that when you make a change, the contractor may not be able to finish your job by the completion date stated in the contract. You and your contractor should discuss this point and, if need be, add an amendment to the contract that changes the completion date.

Insurance Coverage

Let's face it: Your home is about to become a construction site, fraught with dangers to people and property, and you'll need to

Know What You're Getting Yourself Into

*F*or every aspect of your remodel, you should always know exactly how much something is going to cost you before you give your contractor the green light to do any work. So before he starts work on any change or addition to the original plans, make sure you get the cost from him in writing—you may be surprised at how much even the smallest change costs!

make sure your contract gives you the proper protections in a variety of scenarios. For example, anyone—a subcontractor working on the job, a visiting neighbor, or even a child who wanders onto your property—can get hurt. And there is also the potential for property damage, either to your home or someone else's. Since there are so many different things that can go wrong, if your contractor is not properly insured, your financial well-being is on the line. As we have said, it is essential that your contractor have in place both worker's compensation insurance (in case of injury to his workers) and liability insurance (in case of injury to anyone else or property damage). If you have the right homeowner's insurance policy, it may cover you, but you don't want to be making claims that could affect your premiums—you'll want your contractor to be responsible. Ideally, your contract should provide that you will be added as an "additional insured" to your contractor's liability insurance policy so that the contractor's insurance will provide the primary coverage in the event you or anyone else has a liability claim in connection with the work. Finally, the contract should state that the contractor will have his insurance company or companies send you insurance certificates showing proof of coverage (that the policy is in full force and effect), the amount of coverage, you as an additional insured, and that the insurance will not be

Don't Rely on Just Him: Have Your Own Insurance, Too

Contact your insurance agent before you start construction. (If you don't have a homeowner's policy, you should get one.) You will want to make sure that your general liability insurance coverage (part of your homeowner's policy) is adequate, and you will also want to speak to your insurance agent to make sure that you have any other coverage you might need to cover your construction.

canceled without you getting prior notice (typically, thirty or forty-five days, depending on the insurance company).

As to the amount of coverage for the contractor's various policies, the coverage for workers' compensation insurance is usually determined by law. You should consult with a financial adviser or attorney about what is a sufficient amount for liability insurance.

Warranties and Guaranties

Construction is a very complicated thing, and so many things can go wrong, even if everyone is doing everything right. Chances are you'll find imperfections, defects, and problems with the work as you live with it. For example, your contractor installs brand-new hardwood flooring. After a few months, you realize that the floors are uneven. You tell your contractor about it and the two of you figure out that the subcontractor did not install the subflooring correctly. Everything needs to be ripped out and redone. But you don't need to pursue the subcontractor yourself; under your warranty from your general contractor he is responsible for fixing it. The typical contract should provide that the contractor will guaranty and warranty his work for at least one year from completion of all the work—not just from completion of that part of the work. And it should be a guaranty of all labor *and* materials. Also, sometimes a manufacturer or a subcontractor's warranty will be of longer duration or of greater scope than the warranty you get from your contractor. Your appliances will also come with warranties. Your contract should make it clear that your contractor's warranty does not limit the longer or better warranties you are entitled to by law or from third parties. Make sure that the contract states that your contractor will assign any third-party warranties and guaranties (like the appliance guaranties) to you so that you have the option of going to the third party—like the appliance manufacturer—for repairs if you need to.

Termination Clauses

We recommend that your contract contain a no-fault termination option. If you don't have one, then you might have to pay termination fees unless you can prove that your contractor is in breach of contract. Like a no-fault divorce, this clause lets you get out of it for any reason—or for no reason—by giving the contractor written notice and paying him for the work he's already done, so you can cut him loose without having to build a case against him. This might not at first seem fair to your contractor, but if you consider Amanda's experience, you'll understand why it's important.

> Amanda wanted to get started on her new room addition right away. But every contractor her architect, Brandon, recommended seemed to be tied up on another project. So when George was available, it seemed like a small miracle. George's work was usually good, but Brandon warned Amanda and her husband, Justin, that George could be temperamental. But nothing prepared Amanda and Justin for George's rudeness and nasty attitude when they tried to ask questions and wanted to make a few changes based on some of their own research and knowledge. And most of George's outbursts were directed at Amanda, even when it was Justin who was voicing most of the concerns. Fortunately, George's construction work on the job was first rate, and all the while he remained on budget and on schedule. But the couple's level of discomfort with George was taking the pleasure out of the entire project, and it soon became unbearable for the couple–particularly for Amanda–to continue to work with George under these conditions. Yet for all his rudeness, because the actual construction work was going so well, it would have been hard to terminate George for breach, because technically he wasn't breaching the contract. However, because their contract provided that they could terminate George for any reason or for no reason, they had an out.

Dispute Resolution

If you get into a fight, most contractors prefer not to go to court, and their contracts usually provide for this. Here are the basic reasons: You probably know that you have the option of suing in court if you and your contractor have a legal disagreement. You very well may have heard horror stories about lawsuits—even from the winners—that might make some of the construction stories you've heard sound pretty tame. Well, contractors have heard them, too, so they, like a lot of people these days, prefer to stay out of court.

In many contracts, both the contractor and owner agree to give up their right to sue each other in court and instead agree to resolve their disputes by other means: mediation and arbitration. Mediation is usually informal; the parties meet with a mediator to see if they can work things out. Because mediation isn't binding, if the parties can't work out their differences, they then go to the next step: arbitration.

Arbitration is like a court proceeding. It is more formal, the parties usually have lawyers, the arbitrator is often a retired judge, and the parties usually agree in advance that the arbitrator's decision will be final and binding on them. The arbitration takes place in a conference room, not a courtroom, at a time and place convenient to the parties. But beware: A lot of lawyers don't like to have their clients give up their rights to go to court, and this can be an individual decision. You should consult with a lawyer if you have any questions about whether to opt for arbitration and give up your right to go to court.

OTHER CONTRACT GOODIES YOU MAY NEED OR WANT

There are a few other provisions that you may need or want in the contract, depending on your situation.

Work to Be Done by Anyone Else

You may end up hiring someone else besides your general contractor to work on your remodel. For example, you may have your own painter or your own carpenter. If you plan to do this, let your contractor know. Make sure your contract acknowledges that you will be hiring these tradesmen, and that he must cooperate with these third parties. Make it clear that your contractor will not receive his fee on work done by your own tradesmen, if he will not be responsible to supervise them or warranty their work.

Financing Contingency

You may have seen this clause before when you purchased your home; you were able to get out of the purchase contract if you couldn't get the loan you wanted. Similarly, if you are planning to finance your remodel with a loan, make sure you can get out of your deal with the contractor if the loan doesn't come through within a certain amount of time.

Cleanup

Remodeling is messy, dirty, dusty, and noisy. And after all the work is done, there is a lot of cleanup to make the space livable and safe. The contract should specify who will handle this. If you are going to live in your home during construction, your contract should obligate the contractor to seal off the work area from your living space, clean up dust and debris as much as possible at the end of each workday, and store materials (tools, supplies, etc.) as safely as possible. Dust control is important if someone in your home has allergies, and these safety precautions are critical if you have young children.

Bathroom Facilities

If you don't want workers tracking construction grime into your bathroom, make sure your contract requires your contractor to provide a portable toilet on site for the crew.

Special Instructions

If you have any special needs—special work hours, safety concerns, security, etc.—don't be shy about putting them into the contract. Note that most localities have regulations dictating when work can start and must end each day, but you may have your own needs.

BEFORE YOU SIGN THE CONTRACT

Make sure you understand everything the contract says and, if you have a lawyer helping you, make sure that he or she has explained everything to you. Another tip: If there are any handwritten changes to the contract, make sure the contractor puts his initials next to them in addition to signing the contract. That way he can't claim that he didn't see them or that they were added after the fact!

10

Assembling the Rest of Your Dream Team:

HIRING AND UNDERSTANDING THE ROLE OF ARCHITECTS, INTERIOR DESIGNERS, ENGINEERS, AND OTHER PROFESSIONALS

*W*HILE YOUR CONTRACTOR may seem like the most important person in your renovation, he might not be the only person you will be seeing during your project, and he might not even be the first person you hire. Sometimes before you even begin your search for a general contractor, you may be hiring a host of other professionals.

Home renovation often calls for the services of a whole cast of characters: architects, interior designers, and engineers, to name a few. The more complex or extensive the project, the more likely it is that you will be hiring a whole team of professionals.

THE INTERIOR DESIGNER:
New Best Friend or Bitchy Diva?

When mention is made of an interior designer, most people think of someone they hire to help out with the fun stuff—picking out paint colors, finishes, hardware, furniture, and tchotchkes. While some women feel incredibly intimidated at the prospect of choosing these things themselves, others wonder why they should spend money for an interior designer when they feel perfectly capable of picking out their own appliances, paint, and knobs. If you are one of those women whose guilty pleasures include hours spent watching HGTV and reading design magazines, you may think you know a lot but you can still benefit from hiring a designer.

What a lot of people don't know is that while designers don't have the same technical background as the architect (you should always have an architect or engineer involved with a project that involves structural issues), many interior designers can do a lot of the same things that an architect can, such as planning architectural elements of the home and drawing up or doing computerized floor plans and elevations. As a result, and depending on the nature of your project, you may not need to hire an architect at all.

And like an architect, a designer usually knows the good contractors out there, and can be very helpful in the selection process if the designer enters the picture before the contractor does.

Anyone can call himself or herself a designer. Some designers have had very little or no formal training at all and simply have a great sense of style and a knack for decorating. Others, though, may have had a great deal of formal training and may even have special training and credentials in kitchen and bathroom design. (A designer with the initials *CBD*

> ## Who Gets Hired First?
>
> There's no magic formula. You may find a contractor first, only to learn from him that you also need to consult with an architect. Or you may first develop a relationship with an architect or designer and that person may help you find a general contractor.

after his or her name is a certified bath designer, and a designer who uses the initials *CKD* is a certified kitchen designer.) Oftentimes, showrooms that display things like kitchen cabinetry and bathroom vanities are owned by designers or have designers on staff with these certifications to help you plan things out.

When you meet with designers, make sure you talk with them about their experience and training and find out what tasks they can and can't handle.

Design Is Always a Matter of Opinion

If you don't see eye to eye on style, color, or clutter, then you won't get along very well with your designer. One of the

---

I'm an Interior Designer: Don't Call Me a Decorator

*I*s there really a distinction? No, there is not. The two terms can be used interchangeably. Many people who call themselves interior designers, though, hate to be called decorators—especially the ones who have had formal training to perform services that are of a quasi-architectural nature. They find the term *decorator* demeaning and they think it implies that all they do is pick out furniture and drapes. It's kind of like the chef who cringes when he is referred to as a *cook*.

---

most important things about selecting the right interior designer is to make sure you pick someone who shares your taste and vision for your home. It's a lot different from dealing with your contractor. Think about it: There is a right way and a wrong way to install a toilet, but the color of the bathroom walls or the type of tile you choose is always a matter of opinion. You should expect even the most professional and experienced designer to have strong opinions and a healthy ego—if you disagree with each other, there can be a lot of hurt feelings all around. So before you hire any designer, be sure to review and discuss the designer's portfolio in great detail.

If we had to generalize, the vast majority of designers fall into one of two categories: New Best Friend or Bitchy Diva. Ideally, your designer (male or female) will be your New Best Friend—the person who will care about your remodel nearly as much as you

Make Some Decisions Off the Clock

With life being as busy as it is, couples might not have time to talk about design decisions before they meet with the designer. One piece of advice: Don't waste money fighting with your partner in front of your designer about tile and cabinets when you can chat (and fight) about these things beforehand. You might not come to an agreement before your meeting and, in fact, you might need your designer's help to break an impasse, but at least you'll save the money that the designer will charge you for listening to the banter.

do and who you will pal around with as you shop, plot, and plan.

Unfortunately, sometimes disputes over style and your designer's bills are unavoidable. This is when you may see the Bitchy Diva side of your New Best Friend. Your designer may ask, "How could you possibly stand to have that crappy old rug in your beautiful home, when everything else is so gorgeous?" Your bank account is already bleeding from your construction costs and your designer wants you to spend $20,000 to replace a perfectly good rug? Well, maybe that just can't happen. And, anyway, you don't think the rug is so bad!

Since many designers can be ego driven and emotional, there may be a lot of attitude coming your way if you don't like your designer's choices. If this happens to you, take a deep breath and set a few boundaries. Remind the designer that this is *your* home and *your* checkbook!

How They Get Paid

Interior designers are usually paid by the hour. They may also receive a markup on anything they buy for you. A designer may also get a retainer, which generally is applied to any hourly fees or markups but sometimes a designer will charge a retainer, which is nonrefundable and nonapplicable.

When a designer quotes you an hourly rate, you may think that it sounds like no big deal compared with the tens or hundreds of thousands of dollars you'll be spending on construction. But you would be surprised at how quickly hourly fees can add up, particularly if your designer is charging you for travel time, time spent shopping (with or without you), and time for meetings and phone calls. So make sure the two of you have a frank chat about money. Find out how much your designer expects things to cost. You can ask your designer to tell you when he or she approaches a particular dollar amount, so you can reevaluate at that point and attempt to keep a lid on costs. Whatever your agreement with the interior designer, as is the case with the contractor, architect, or other professionals you hire, get it in writing.

THE ARCHITECT:
Artist and Master Planner

If you are taking down walls, reconfiguring spaces, or building a second story or an addition, then you very well may want to hire an architect. (Remember, as we said in Chapter 7, you also have the option of hiring a design/build firm.) An architect is trained in the art and science of conceiving and drawing up plans, integrating the old and the new, ensuring that everything is designed to be safe, and making sure the design is practical.

An architect's savvy can also be invaluable for restoring or adding to an architecturally or historically distinct house. Although there are contractors out there who have an artistic flair and sense of architectural style, their main specialty is to coordinate and manage the construction.

While contractors, as a group, tend to get a bad rap, architects generally have a better reputation. It's not that all architects are angels, but they do tend to be highly professional. Particularly on a complex project, the architect will often play a critical role in identifying and helping you solve problems, figuring out whether you need to hire engineers and other specialists, and possibly even doing the matchmaking—helping you select the perfect contractor for the job. Even so, you'll want to have a written agreement with your architect specifying services and fees.

Choosing an Architect

When choosing an architect, as is the case with the contractor, it's a good idea to interview several. You'll want to see pictures of projects the architect has worked on, and it's important that you and your architect are on the same page before plans are drawn up. This is not to say that he or she has to agree with you right away about everything you think you want to do. "Your wish is my command" is not what you should be after here. Architects frequently come up with great ideas that will only enhance a project. They'll also point out flaws in your vision if they see them. On the other hand, if you think an architect simply doesn't get what you want to do or isn't listening, it's time to keep interviewing.

Is Your Home the Architect's Type?

Many architects specialize in a particular style or a few styles. If your home is a traditional colonial home and you want to keep it that way, then you probably will not be best served by hiring an architect renowned for his or her modern design innovations. And you're not likely to get plans for an Italian villa from an architect who specializes in the retro styles of the 1950s and 1960s.

How Involved Will the Architect Be?

Sometimes architects simply prepare plans and construction documents (called *Plans and Specs*) for the contractor to use to build the project, and this can often suffice when the remodel is a smaller project, such as the renovation of a couple of rooms. But for the more complex projects, the architect can provide far more extensive services, such as assisting with cost estimates, making sure the project complies with building codes, overseeing the project during construction, and acting as the team captain. The architect can also be someone you turn to when the going gets rough—and we're not just talking about having a shoulder to cry on! An architect can often help in resolving issues that come up with the contractor.

The Five Phases of Architectural Services

On a big job, architectural services are divided into five phases.

- **Schematic design phase**. This is when the architect prepares rough drawings of basic concepts. You might find, at this stage, that you and the architect don't see eye to eye on the project. If this is the case, you can give the architect your comments and have him or her attempt to redo the basic design. If after a couple of tries it seems that the architect just doesn't get your vision, then you should consider paying the architect an hourly fee for the work already done and moving on to another architect.

- **Design development phase**. At this stage, the architect will give you a lot more detail, such as showing the structural systems; the heating and air-conditioning systems; and the electrical, plumbing, and communications systems. These plans should have sufficient detail to allow you to get a preliminary cost estimate, but they typically won't have quite enough detail to allow the contractor to build the project. With this information, you can assess whether your budget is truly on the right track. Make sure you get cost estimates no later than at this stage—you must make sure your architect is designing a project you can afford to build!

- **Construction documents phase**. This is when the architect prepares detailed drawings that the contractor can build from. On a big project, a contractor should bid the project based on construction documents only.

- **Bidding and negotiating phase**. If you haven't already chosen your contractor, this is the stage at which the architect can help you chose a contractor by assisting you in the bidding process and/or in negotiating your contractor's proposal and contract.

- **Construction phase.** Once construction commences, the architect's adminstrative work begins, provided the two of you have agreed that the architect will be involved in this way. The architect will attend the site meetings, which will often be weekly for a major remodel, once things are in full swing. You may also want to have the architect involved in looking over the contractor's invoices (sometimes called applications for payment) to make sure the contractor has completed all the work, obtained all the materials for which he is requesting payment, and to make sure that the work was done correctly. If it's not, then you'll be able to withhold payment for the items in question until completed.

The Architect's Fee

An architect can offer services on an hourly basis, and this is often how an architect is paid on a small project. However, on a larger project or when an architect performs the full range of services described above, the architect's compensation is often based on a percentage of the cost of the project. The percentage that architects charge can vary, depending on where you live and how in demand your architect is. Additional services not in the original contract (like redoing the plans if you change your mind about things) are usually billed hourly, and there is often a markup on reimbursable expenses, such as costs for printing and copying plans, and travel.

When Payment Gets Made

On a small job, the architect will typically invoice hourly fees on a monthly basis. On a big job for which the architect performs an extensive array of services (as described above) and is paid on a percentage basis, the construction costs are estimated ahead of time for the purpose of estimating the fee. For example, if the construction costs are estimated at $200,000, and if the architect charges a fee of 15 percent, then the total estimated fee will be

$30,000. This fee typically is paid progressively and invoiced monthly when the architect is rendering services. So, if the architect thinks schematic designs will take three months, then the fee for this stage will be paid out in thirds over the three-month period. As construction costs change, the amounts due to the architect at each stage are adjusted, with any unpaid amounts for a prior stage due and payable immediately. Here is how a typical payment schedule would work:

- **Schematic design:** Payment is 10 percent of the architect's total fee.

- **Design development:** Payment is 15 percent of the architect's total fee. If there is no schematic design phase, then payment is 25 percent of the fee by the end of the design development stage.

- **Construction documents:** Payment is 40 percent of the architect's total fee; this is when the architect is putting in the most time doing very detailed plans.

- **Bidding and negotiating:** Payment is 5 percent of the architect's total fee. If the architect does not help you with the bidding process, then this percentage can be added onto the next phase.

- **Construction administration:** Payment is the remaining 30 percent of the architect's total fee.

Insurance

As you probably know, doctors and lawyers can be sued for malpractice if they do something wrong. The same is true for architects. This is why it's a good idea to hire an architect who carries malpractice insurance, also called professional liability insurance or errors and omissions insurance. The same holds true when hiring structural engineers. You should know that many architects and structural engineers do not carry this type of insurance because the premiums are high. If you hire one of these professionals with the knowledge that they don't have insurance, that is the risk you take.

THE OUTDOORSY TYPES:
The Landscape Architect and Landscape Contractor

Outdoor renovations, especially if they are extensive, often call for the expertise of a landscape architect. Many landscape architects are trained in all aspects of designing outdoor space, not just the foliage, but also the location of patios, walkways, outdoor structures, and other outdoor features. While it is more common to hire a landscape architect to design an elaborate outdoor plan, any size space can benefit from a beautiful landscape design. A landscape architect can make sure that a small outdoor space is used efficiently. Just as is the case when hiring an architect or designer, it is important that you and the landscape architect share a vision for your outdoor space. For example, you may not want to hire one who is known for designing English gardens if what you are looking for is a tropical paradise. Be sure that you review the landscape architect's portfolio, check references, and get several bids.

Some landscape architects are like design/build firms in that, in addition to doing the design, they have a crew of subcontractors who handle the building and installation of various elements of the project, such as hardscape, decking, pools, and landscaping. Other times, you will have to hire a separate landscape contractor (or several different contractors, like a pool contractor and deck installer) to implement the landscape architect's plans. For an extensive outdoor renovation, you will want to have a contract with the landscape contractor with many of the same bells and whistles as the construction contract with your general contractor.

THE GEEK SQUAD:
Surveyors and Engineers

Surveyors and engineers are brought in to perform specialized services for your project. The average person doesn't usually know when to hire a surveyor or an engineer. So if you need one, your designer, architect, or contractor will let you know.

Like the IT guy at work or that genius in your tenth-grade math class, the surveyor or engineer on your project will often communicate in technical jargon that the average person typically doesn't understand, so don't feel intimidated if you don't either. Instead, ask for clarification or, if necessary, get a translation from your designer, architect, or contractor.

Surveyor

A survey is a professional drawing by a licensed surveyor showing where things are located on your property. If you are just renovating the interior of your home, it is extremely unlikely that you'll need a surveyor. But if your renovation involves new additions, additional structures, or any other change on your land, you may need one. The most important thing a survey will show is the current location of buildings, fences, and other structures as well as the boundaries of your land and the locations of easements. (An easement is a right a third party has to use your property. An example of a typical easement would be the right of a utility company to install and maintain an underground sewer line on your property. Another example of an easement would be the right of your next-door neighbor to drive over the driveway leading to his property that happens to be located on your land.) For an extra fee, a survey can also show more detail, such as elevations. Lucky for you, you probably aren't going to need to decide what your survey is going to show. Your architect or contractor will order the survey and tell the surveyor what to draw. The only thing you'll have to do is pay for it!

Structural Engineer

You may need to hire a structural engineer if your project involves changing or building any load-bearing or other structure. Examples of when you might need to hire a structural engineer are when you take down a load-bearing wall or build a second story. As we said earlier in this chapter, check to see if the structural engineer carries malpractice insurance.

Geologists and Soils Engineers

Soil isn't something most people ordinarily think about when making changes to anything other than their lawns, but its condition could be critical to your project. Now we aren't talking about landscaping; we mean the kind of soil on which your home sits. Depending on where you live, you might need to hire one of these professionals to do reports and tests to see if you can build what you want to build or change your home the way you want to change it. You should consider consulting with a geologist or soils engineer if your property is located on a hillside, if you have persistent drainage problems, if your property is located in earthquake country, if your house is in an area prone to mudslides or flooding, if your house is located close to the water, or if your house is built on sandy soil.

THE EXPEDITOR:
Your Own Knight in Shining Armor

Just as you are getting your mind around the details of your project, you might find yourself faced with the frustrating reality that something about your property, project, or plans is slowing down the governmental approval process. You may need extra help. You might want to hire an expeditor and you should discuss this option with your contractor.

Expeditors are usually former inspectors who really know the ropes. They are like ambassadors-for-hire: They plead and negotiate your case before the building department and navigate the twists and turns of the often-complex approval process. They can let you know whether your plans and expectations are realistic. And since they are former inspectors, they have instant credibility when they meet with current inspectors on your behalf. Sure it's an additional expense; but for a complex project, the savings in time, money, and aggravation can translate into money well spent.

11

Why Can't We All Just Get Along?

PREVENTING AND DEALING WITH CONSTRUCTION DRAMA

*F*OR ANY PROJECT—large or small—you should expect that there will be bumps along the way. If you know what to expect, then you'll know how to deal with the all-but-inevitable problems before things blow up in a way that could derail the whole affair. In this chapter, we give you some tips on how to manage your expectations. We show you how you can keep yourself in check so things don't escalate. We let you know when you should kiss and make up with members of your team if things have gotten a little ugly, and we shed some light on when it might be time to cut your losses and move on.

GETTING A GRIP ON YOUR EXPECTATIONS

You are now embarking on a high-stakes relationship with your contractor and other professionals you may be hiring. On your side of the equation, they are in your house and in your wallet. On their side, if you are not happy with them, you may not pay them. And as stressful as remodeling is in the best of circumstances, the last thing you want to do is complicate the situation by having unrealistic expectations.

Because a remodel entails so many details, you should expect that things will not go perfectly. This is not to excuse incompetence or mismanagement by your contractor, or anyone else for that matter. But keep in mind that things can go wrong even when everyone is on top of everything. And although you may be upset by delays or by having to spend more money, not every problem is always someone else's fault. So don't go nuts the minute something goes wrong. How all of you handle problems that come up along the way can be the difference between a great working relationship and an intolerable one.

Not Everything Is an Emergency

Once the job is under way, you'll be seeing a lot of your contractor and his crew. Things will be much better if there is mutual respect and cooperation. You will need to talk to your contractor a lot, but that doesn't mean you have to call him every five minutes. He'll probably be a lot more responsive if he doesn't perceive you as being overly needy.

Weekly Meetings and Coordinating Your Schedules

In Chapter 9, we explained how useful it is to have regular meetings with your contractor. We cannot emphasize enough how important this is. These meetings will often include, in addition to your contractor, other people involved with your job (such as your designer, architect, or a particular tradesman), depending on the stage of the project.

If you don't see your contractor in person regularly, find out what the best times are to talk to him on the phone. Contractors usually start working pretty early in the morning and tend to end their workday by late afternoon. It might be easier for him to talk to you when he's on his way to the job site, or it might be better for him in the evening after he's done his rounds for the day. You should also make sure he knows the best and worst times to reach you. For example, if you're getting young kids off to school in the morning and they'll be screaming in the background when you're on the phone, maybe you're better off having conversations with your contractor after they've left. Or if you typically have early morning meetings at work, maybe the afternoon is a better time to touch base.

Keep Up Your End of the Bargain

You are counting on your team for a lot, but they are counting on you, too. This doesn't just mean your showing up for meetings or paying on time. It also means getting your contractor the materials or items that are your responsibility and making design decisions in a timely fashion so that you are not the source of any delays. And don't forget to take care of the little things that make your contractor's life easier, like making sure you've cleared your driveway for the delivery van or remembering not to park in front of your house the day the contractor brings by the Dumpster.

WE NEED TO TALK:
Trying to Work with Your Contractor When Things Go Wrong

With emotions running high, it's easy to flip out when something goes awry. One word of advice: *don't*. Don't scream or yell. Do take a deep breath before you get into it. Do try to be reasonable. Remind yourself (again and again) that no one can control things like bad weather and delivery delays. So, when problems arise, take a step back from the situation and ask yourself the following questions.

Whose Fault Is It?

The two most common problems that arise in any project are that it falls behind schedule and that it goes over budget. These things can happen for any number of reasons. Your contractor might not have been able to do much work because it rained nonstop for a month. Or perhaps you ended up making a lot of changes to your plans or project. Your contractor is not responsible for these things. But your contractor is responsible if he has his subs tied up on other jobs or failed to order those windows when he said he would. It's a delicate thing—figuring out who is at fault or figuring out that no one is at fault. Instead of ripping into your contractor, try to reach the best solution. If your contractor is at fault, the important thing is that he takes responsibility and fixes the problem.

Is There a Perfect Fix?

There are times when there is no perfect solution to a mistake. Even when the contractor takes responsibility and does what needs to be done, correcting the problem may delay the project. You may just have to grit your teeth and try to get past your frustration at your project not being completed when you thought it would be.

What If You Don't Like One of the Subs?

There are many possible reasons why you may feel uncomfortable with one of the subcontractors on the job. It could be that he doesn't show up on time, disappears for hours, behaves inappropriately, or that you just don't like his work. Whatever the reason may be, if you are unhappy or concerned, you should speak to your contractor about it immediately.

Is Your Contractor Too Busy?

Your contractor may have promised you that he wouldn't take other jobs or that you would always be his top priority. You're not the first woman he's fed this line to, and you won't be the last. The truth is, your contractor will almost always be seeing other people. Other people's jobs can be a major reason for delays on yours, because his attention, subs, or other resources are elsewhere. So, if your contractor is suddenly less available than he used to be, you might have to confront him to get him back on track.

What If Your Contractor Is Not Listening to You?

You may find that you and your contractor get along well enough when things are going well but that he just doesn't seem to listen to you when the going gets a little tough. He may be the type of man who doesn't like dealing with or taking instructions from a woman. In this day and age, while few men will come right out and say it, unfortunately, some are still thinking it, and you may see it in his actions. You may also find that you and your contractor seem to butt heads on a regular basis for one reason or another.

One great strategy for working things out with your contractor is to involve someone else who can bring a different dynamic to the table. When you are remodeling with a spouse or partner you may decide to play the game of good cop/bad cop. One of you can be the tough one, and the other can be the friendlier one or the voice of reason. But even if you are remodeling alone, there is no reason you also can't work this strategy. You can try bringing along a family member or a good friend . . . anyone who gets it and can talk to your contractor when the need arises. If you're bringing in someone who is not a partner, spouse, or someone directly involved with the project, your contractor may feel like he is being ganged up on, but if you are able to deal with him more effectively this way, then he may just have to deal with it.

It is also very common to enlist the help of your designer or architect (if you have one) to try to resolve disputes with your contractor. In fact, it is so common that many contracts have clauses that actually provide for the architect or designer to step into this role.

WHO'S RUNNING THIS SHOW?

If you know that you will have a number of people involved with your project, you are probably asking yourself which of your team members will be taking the lead. The answer is: There is no right answer. Your contractor may seem like the obvious person, but you may gravitate toward someone else—usually the person you work with the most or have come to trust the most. Sometimes, particularly on a large job, the architect will run the show, helping you prepare the plans, bid the job, and hire the contractor and other professionals. Other times, your designer will be the person you bond with and want to take charge; the designer might even hire the architect for structural matters and recommend the contractor.

Whoever takes the lead, it is important that each of your team members not only gets along with you but also gets along with everybody else on the team—at least most of the time anyway. But as things go, it's not uncommon to have personality conflicts and blame thrown around if and when problems arise. Ideally, you want to avoid being dragged into the middle of any disagreements, but sometimes it's unavoidable. Throughout this book, we give suggestions about dealing with particular problems. Having regular meetings with your team can be very helpful when something needs to be smoothed out. And one more thing: Remember to bring the doughnuts!

BREAKUPS AND WHEN YOU MAY NEED TO TALK TO A LAWYER

Anyone undergoing a home renovation dreads the possibility of the contractor checking out, right in the middle of the process. He may stop paying his subs, he could stop showing up, or he might just seem to have stopped paying attention. Soon, the job is falling behind schedule. This could happen for many reasons. Often, it's because the contractor has run into financial problems.

Sometimes small problems are symptoms of larger ones. Trust your instincts if you think something is wrong. But don't beat yourself up if you don't find out about problems right away. After all, a dishonest contractor or one with financial difficulties will go to great lengths to hide a problem. You may not know that he hasn't paid his subs until they either show up on your doorstep one day asking for money and threatening to put a lien on your home or stop showing up altogether.

If the problem is not so bad, such as the contractor missing a few days of work here and there, a conversation to get things back on track may be all it takes. But if your contractor is incompetent, fails to pay his subs, or does shoddy work, then firing him is probably the right decision.

If you are at the very beginning stages of your project, making a decision to fire your contractor may not be such a big deal, especially if you can find a good contractor to step in. But if you are already well into the project, firing him should be the decision of last resort since changing contractors midstream is difficult. You're virtually guaranteed that your project will be delayed, that you'll have to get bids all over again, and that you'll have to reassess your budget. Also, many contractors are reluctant to pick up where another contractor has left off, so you might have trouble finding someone good to take over and finish up.

Some contracts allow you to get out of the relationship without paying termination fees even if the contractor isn't at fault. Still, it's a good idea to talk to a lawyer to make sure you know your rights and obligations in this touchy situation.

As for working with architects and designers, the most common problem that arises is finding out that you are not on the same page, either with respect to your vision of the project or the budget. You can try to come to a meeting of the minds, but there are situations in which it becomes necessary to part ways and move on.

PART 3

Shopping for Your Remodel and Surviving Construction

12

Shop Till You Drop:
HOW A WOMAN'S FAVORITE HOBBY CAN TURN HER INTO A SAVVY CONSTRUCTION CONSUMER

*Y*OU ARE ABOUT to embark on one of the biggest extended shopping sprees of your life . . . and we know you'll be up to the challenge! Don't let anyone tell you that all those hours at the mall, on eBay, or window shopping have been a waste of your time. They haven't just been idle hours of fun. After all, looking for that perfect kitchen faucet to match those exquisite knobs is no different from the search for a new pair of shoes to go with that new dress you just bought. Shopping at those incredible after-Christmas sales was just a warmup . . . soon you'll be cruising every stone yard, tile store, and kitchen-design showroom in town like a pro, learning what's out there and what's in vogue, finding what you like, and getting yourself the best deals you can.

As any experienced shopper knows, it's not just about getting the least expensive thing. It's more about your sense of style, what works best for you, and getting what you want for the best value. The cheapest appliances might save you a few dollars in the short run, but they will cost you time, money and aggravation in the long run if they wear out just as their warranties expire. And if that oven doesn't have the features you want, was it really such a bargain? Better to get the best price for what you really need and want.

SHOULD YOU BUY THROUGH YOUR CONTRACTOR OR DESIGNER, OR CUT YOUR OWN DEALS?

You might be tempted to avoid your contractor's or designer's markup by buying certain things on your own. This may or may not save you money. Keep in mind that many of the best vendors and material suppliers give contractors and designers deep discounts that they just won't give to the general public. So even with a markup, your contractor or designer might still be getting you a better price than you could get on your own. If you openly discuss your shopping intentions, your contractor or designer may be willing to split discounts and reduce markups so that the deal becomes a better one.

THE BEST THINGS TO SHOP FOR ON YOUR OWN

Some of the best things to shop for on your own are appliances, kitchen cabinets (if you're not using a cabinet maker), bathroom and kitchen fixtures (such as sinks, tubs, showers, and faucets), hardware, tile, stone, countertop materials, and light fixtures. Your contractor or designer can steer you in the right direction . . . and so can we.

Bathroom and Kitchen Fixtures and Cabinets

There are many specialty stores devoted to bathrooms and kitchens. Some sell a variety of bath and kitchen items, such as fixtures, hardware, and cabinetry, whereas others may specialize in just one of these categories. Many of these stores are either owned by or have on-staff certified bath or certified kitchen designers who can help plan your kitchen or bathroom remodel. These people can draw up plans after coming to your home to take measurements. Some warehouse stores also have in-house designers who can create the plans for you, if you have not engaged your own architect or designer.

Appliances

Shopping for appliances can be one of the most fun things to do during your remodel. There are so many great choices and features. Some department stores sell appliances, and you can also find appliances at warehouse, electronic, retail, and specialty stores. One of the best places to go shopping are the big appliance warehouses, some of which have full kitchen displays so you can see what the appliances look like in a real setup. But before you run around to every warehouse in town, go online and look in magazines to see what's available, what you like, and what's most energy efficient. Be sure to talk to your contractor and your designer about what will work in your home.

Hardware

Many designers refer to the hardware that adorns your home—knobs, handles, locks, and the like—as your home's jewelry. There is a wide selection of styles and finishes to choose from (antique nickel, oil-rubbed bronze, and aged copper, just to name a few). At specialty stores, you can get great hardware, but it may be a bit pricey. Many similar items are available at a fraction of the cost at home warehouse stores, chain retailers, or online. Also, if you have some expensive hardware you want to keep from your home (such as good-quality locks) but want it to match the new stuff, there are places that will refinish or replate these kinds of things for you. It can be a lot cheaper than buying new.

Tile

It's hard to know where to begin when shopping for tile. It's easy to get overwhelmed by the array of choices. So, if you don't know what you're looking for, one of the most important things to look for in a tile store (in addition to it having competitive prices) is a display that somehow makes it feel manageable. Many people assume that tile—whether for floors or countertops—is less expensive than other materials such as stone. This is not necessarily true. One of the biggest factors in tile pricing is whether the tile is machine or man-made. Handmade tile tends to be much more expensive than machine made, and beautiful hand-painted tile can be more expensive than many natural stones or other materials (see Chapter 14).

Stone

The best place to go shopping for stone is a stone yard. Visiting a stone yard is like going to an abstract art exhibit. Granite and marble, in particular, are available in many different colors and patterns, which, when seen in slab form, can be magnificent to view. When you buy stone, if it's in slab form, make sure you buy consecutive pieces so that the color, grain, and pattern match. With stone tile you may also want to make sure that it is all from the same lot if it's important to you that there is not noticeable variation in color. If you just need a small piece of stone (for example, for a bathroom counter), you probably don't need to buy a whole slab. Most stone yards and stone stores have pieces of broken slabs that they will sell for a fraction of the cost. Small, broken or remainder pieces may be in a back room somewhere, so ask about them if you don't see them.

THE RULES OF SHOPPING FOR YOUR REMODEL

In some ways, shopping for your remodel will be just like shopping for anything else. Most of us are used to going into a store and paying whatever the price tag says. Sure, you might wait for that great bag to go on sale or check out another store to compare prices, but it's not like you can cut a deal with the sales clerk at your favorite shoe store for those fabulous boots. This may be the way it goes when shopping for things like appliances. Sometimes, the best you can do is comparison shop store to store. With other things, though, you should have a different game plan:

- **Bat those eyelashes and bargain away.** When it comes to shopping for your remodel, there are certain venues—stone yards, for example—where not only can you bargain but the vendor doesn't expect experienced shoppers to accept or pay the first price quoted. In fact, if you don't bargain, chances are you'll get ripped off. So remember to bring your feminine wiles and your bargaining smarts with you when you're out shopping. It can't hurt!

- **Sometimes it's better to try it on first.** While certain things are fine to buy online (such as knobs and other hardware), there are other things that you should always see in person before you buy them, such as appliances.

- **Always check return policies.** If you buy anything online or from a catalog, make sure you are dealing with a reputable vendor and can return it if you don't like it. That's because, without seeing something in person, you can never be sure you'll like how it looks or that it will be the right fit.

- **Make calculated splurges.** You may splurge on an outfit once in a while, but may be a budget shopper when it comes to the rest of your wardrobe. If you have a limited remodeling budget, use the same strategy. Spend the most money for the important rooms or the things you really care about.

- **Don't forget about getting something custom made.** Sometimes, the only way you can get what you want is to have it custom made. If you need to repair or want to match something with materials or items that are no longer made, it may even be the cheaper way to go, rather than ripping out everything and starting from scratch. Windows, doors and molding are all examples of things that can be custom made.

- **So what if they're fake?** Authentic antique lighting, faucets, or hardware can be very expensive and out of your price range. But quality reproductions can be reasonably priced. Good reproductions are a lot like good costume jewelry—other people will fall in love with what you have, ask you where you got it, and no one will ever know the difference!

- **Sometimes all it takes is having one great signature piece.** Some fashion aficionados believe it's all about having one amazing accessory to make an outfit or a statement. The rest can be relatively simple and inexpensive. It's the same with a remodel. Even if you don't have a big budget, you may want to splurge on that one thing that will be the centerpiece of a room. A Viking range in a simple kitchen can be like a fabulous piece of jewelry worn with jeans and a T-shirt. Sometimes, that's all it takes to look great.

- **You don't have to go to the most expensive store to get what you want.** Before you splurge on something you have your heart set on, if you are at all concerned with saving money (and who isn't?), take the time to look at similar, less-expensive versions. You'll often be able to find a less expensive alternative that is every bit as attractive and stylish.

- **Man-made materials are not necessarily cheaper.** Don't assume that all synthetic materials are going to be less expensive than natural materials. For example, some popular man-made materials used for countertops can cost more than many marbles or granites. Similarly, a concrete fireplace mantle can run you more than a wood, brick, or stone one.

- **Get the whole truth about price.** When your contractor or designer quotes you a price, it should include the final installed cost and should be covered by the contractor's or manufacturer's warranty. But when shopping on your own for appliances, fixtures, flooring, or other items, the vendor will often quote you the cost of the materials only. So when you buy something, make sure you find out exactly what it's going to cost you. Find out if the store delivers and, if it does, how much delivery will cost. If you have to make your own arrangements, then you will need to figure out who will be responsible if damage occurs in transport. You might have to buy insurance from the delivery service, particularly if you are using a third-party shipper or delivery service. (If you arrange to have your contractor pick something up that you have purchased, make sure you agree ahead of time about whether he will be responsible for the handling of the materials.)

- **It's always a good idea to get a second opinion.** When shopping for clothes, women always want another set of eyes to make sure something looks flattering. That's why you ask your friends, "Does this make me look fat?" Similarly, when remodeling, you may want to ask your contractor or designer to tell you if something you're thinking of buying fits into your home.

You Can't Always Get What You Want

Sometimes items that you want aren't available on your timetable or aren't available at all, no matter how many stores you've called or how extensively you've looked around. That marble flooring you want may take months to ship from Italy, long after your floors have to be in. The one local dealer that carries the clawfoot bathtub you have your heart set on may have sold the last one in stock and won't get another one in any time soon. If you can't get it when you need it, you might be better off just moving on.

13

While You Are Waiting:
THINGS YOU NEED TO HAVE IN PLACE BEFORE WORK BEGINS

*E*XCUSE ME, Mr. Contractor, why is it taking so long to get started?" After weeks or months of planning your remodel, you can't help but feel impatient for the work to begin. Everything, it seems, can slow you down: permits, city approvals, approvals of homeowner's associations, and waiting for materials and subcontractors. But don't get mad—get going! There are a lot of things you can and should be doing before a hammer ever hits a nail.

THE PREPARATION CHECKLIST

Doing Your Shopping

Make sure you get what you need by the time you need it. It's never too early to speak to your contractor or designer about when to order various items and materials you'll need so that they will arrive by the time they have to be installed.

Hooking Up Your Utilities

Speak to your contractor about what utilities or temporary hookups you will need. Notify your gas, water, electric, and cable television companies. You might have to shut off the electricity, water, and gas before you get going. If you have any questions, utility company representatives can often advise you.

Pest Extermination

If you think you have a pest problem, now would be a good time to deal with it. See Chapter 4 for more information, including the possibility of damage to your roof if you choose to tent your home while fumigating.

Insurance

As we said, make sure your contractor has the right insurance policies in place. And make sure *you* have the proper insurance. If you are financing your project with a construction loan, your lender may require it. Consult with your homeowner's insurance carrier or insurance broker about exactly what additional insurance you will need to protect yourself.

Install Phone Lines

Have a telephone (land line) hooked up in the home. We recommend this even in this day and age of cell phones and even if you get good cell phone reception at your job site. (Yes, get used to calling your home a job site!) Your contractor, tradesmen, and subcontractors need to be reachable. Make sure at least one phone at the house does not need electricity—there may be times when the power has to be shut off.

Security First

Whether you will be living in your home during remodeling or not, you must consider various security issues. If you will not be living in your home, then the whole structure will have to be secured. This is important since, as work progresses, materials and fixtures will be delivered and stored at the site. Among other safety precautions, it is a good idea to make sure your property is well lit. Unfortunately, contractors are not always as organized or security conscious as you would expect. So, as deliveries of materials, parts, fixtures, and appliances arrive before and as work progresses, discuss with your contractor having a designated area in the home for these items to be stored such as a locked shed, locked garage, or secured room in the home. If you will be living in your home during a partial remodel, any part of the home that has been opened up will have to be secured, and you will want to make sure you protect your belongings from dust, damage, or theft.

Beware of the Insider

Do not be lulled into a false sense of security because you trust your contractor. Remember that there will be many workers coming in and out of your home. Inside jobs are one of the most common ways that valuables are stolen. Jewelry, watches, cameras, artwork, laptop computers, and other valuable possessions should be carefully stored away, preferably off site and out of sight. Plus, change all your locks and reevaluate your security system when the project is completed; often the insider will keep a key or learn the flaws in your security system so he or she can get access to your stuff later.

Privacy

If you will be living in your home during your remodel, you certainly do not want to have contractors letting themselves in at any hour of the day. (There's little worse than stepping out of the shower to a houseful of tradesmen!) And yet, you may not always be there to open the door. Make access arrangements with your general contractor or construction supervisor. Be very clear about who may and may not have access, who may and may not have the key, and what hours of the day work will begin and end. If you do not have a general contractor, you will have to consider what type of arrangement you feel comfortable making given your circumstances.

Supplies You'll Need at the Construction Site

There's no place like home . . . even one that is under construction. It doesn't matter that you are not living there, your construction site should be conducive to your visits. So bring a roll of toilet paper, paper towels, some bottles of water, a table and chairs, paper and pens, and anything else you think you will need for site meetings, visits, or just hanging out to watch the paint dry.

Staying Friends with the Neighbors

You may not be the only one who has to go through the trials and tribulations of your remodel—if you have neighbors nearby, they may be affected, too. You may have a large, ugly Dumpster sitting on the street for a while and lots of trucks parked there that make driving down your street a tighter squeeze. The work also often generates a lot of noise and sometimes the workers bring their own radios and play loud music. Cigarette butts and other garbage left on neighbors' property will also really tick them off! Make sure you talk to your contractor about these concerns and also let him know that his workers should not block anyone's mailbox, driveway, or garbage bins. It is also not a bad idea to knock on your neighbors' doors or leave a note to let each of them know ahead of time that you will be remodeling.

Planning for Special Installations

Any wires or cables that need to run through walls are installed fairly early on in the construction process. This includes wiring for your security system, doorbell, intercom system, phones, cable, satellite, computer, and speakers for music. Be sure you plan for this work to be done in advance if it's not being handled by your contractor.

WHEN YOU NEED A PERMIT, AND WHAT IT TAKES TO GET ONE

One thing that may be holding up the work is waiting for permits to be issued, as required by local building codes or zoning ordinances. From where you are sitting, these codes and ordinances are nothing but a barrier between you and your project. Although they may be annoying, these codes create important building standards for safety. They also address various neighborhood considerations, such as how high exterior walls can be built and how far from the street homes must be set back.

Whether or not you need a permit for your work depends on where you live and the type of work you are doing. Most every county, city, and town has its own codes and regulations. The general rule, though, is that most major modifications to structures or systems in your home require permits. For an extensive remodel, your contractor may obtain a general building permit covering all of the items you will be working on. For a smaller remodel, you may have to get individual permits for things like electrical or plumbing work.

As soon as you decide on the scope of your work, you should speak to your contractor about whether you'll need a permit to commence work and what it will take to obtain one.

Depending on your project, here are some instances when you can expect a permit to be required:

- Remodeling a bathroom
- Remodeling a kitchen
- Building an addition
- Installing heating and air-conditioning
- Adding an enclosed patio
- Electrical work
- Plumbing work
- Structural demolition
- Moving or removing interior walls

- Remodeling an entire room
- Building or replacing a deck
- Building boundary walls above a certain height
- Foundation work
- Fireplace/chimney work
- Building retaining walls

Depending on the work for which the permit is issued and the issuing office, an inspector will usually inspect the work at certain stages and, generally, at its completion. This is called getting the sign-off on the permit. For example, electrical work will be inspected before and after the walls are closed up. The same is true for plumbing work. Generally speaking, each tradesman is required to get a final sign-off for his work. For larger projects, for which your contractor has gotten a general building permit, he will also need to get a final sign-off for the entire project.

If you are building from the ground up or making major renovations, you may need to obtain a certificate of occupancy (C of O) that will allow you to move back in and occupy the home. You can often get a temporary certificate of occupancy that will allow you to move in before you get the final certificate of occupancy if the home is deemed habitable.

The Dangers of Not Having a Required Permit

Don't get busted! If the relevant governmental authority requires a permit, get one. And make sure your contractor gets the final sign-off. The same goes for the C of O; make sure you get the final one. If you do not follow these regulations and decide to do the work without a permit or you or your contractor does not follow through with getting the final sign-off, you could run into problems down the road. Any inspector who gets wind of your project (either because he or she just happens to pass by or because an irritable neighbor busts you) can slap you with fines and compliance orders. Also, should the remodeling bug bite again, you may have a difficult time getting permits for the new job when you have done previously non-permitted work (at this point, it is likely that you'll be hit with compliance orders and, possibly, fines). You could run into yet another problem when you go to sell your home: Buyers often do not want to purchase property with nonpermitted improvements.

If fears of fines or decreased property values don't persuade you to build with a permit, then perhaps this will: Contractors who fail to build to code are often just the sort to do shoddy work, whereas a reputable contractor will not want to do nonpermitted work. So it may cost you more at the outset to engineer, design, and build your project with proper permits; but in the long run the potential cost and extra time necessary to correct construction flaws, defects, and noncomplying work, surely will be much higher.

We know this all sounds daunting, but getting the required permits does not necessarily have to be such a big deal. Speak to your contractor about what can be done to expedite the process. For example, some building departments have walk-through lines that issue permits on the spot with the submission of the appropriate paperwork and plans.

The best thing to do is to make sure your contractor takes responsibility for obtaining the required permits and sign-offs (see Chapter 9). And make sure he delivers copies or originals of final permits and the C of O to *you*. Do not rely on the relevant governmental authority to keep your permits on file. Even when it keeps good and up-to-date public records (and many do not), it is ultimately the homeowner's responsibility to prove that she has obtained permits and a C of O for her project. And remember what we said earlier: Keep your contractor on his toes! We strongly recommend that you not pay your contractor the full fee until you obtain the final permits and C of O. This can be made a condition of your original contract.

A Little Charm Can Go a Long Way

Do not underestimate the power of turning on the charm with your building inspector. You are at his or her mercy so it pays to be friendly if you are around during an inspection. (Diet Coke or snacks, anyone?) It also can't hurt if your contractor knows the inspector or the people behind the counter.

Not All Work Requires a Permit

Permits are generally not required for these improvements (although, again, different locations have different requirements and you should always check just to make sure *before* you start your project):

- Painting
- Wallpapering
- Finish carpentry work (which includes such things as molding, paneling, and wainscoting)
- Refinishing wood floors
- Most cabinetry work
- Fencing (in most jurisdictions fencing must be under a certain height and in some areas at a specified setback; anything higher or not set back enough requires a variance from the applicable zoning or building code)

Do You Need an Expeditor?

If your plans are complex or you're in a rush, it might not be a bad idea to hire one (see Chapter 11).

WHAT IF YOU CHANGE YOUR PLANS?

We said this before and we'll say it again: No matter how carefully you plan, things change. It's not just because you will change your mind. It's also because you can never really know everything you'll need to do until work starts. You'll probably have a number of change orders. Just remember that this can mean amended plans and amended permits along with additional inspections, and that, in turn, can lead to even more delays.

What to Expect When You Are Building:

THE THREE TRIMESTERS OF CONSTRUCTION

WHEN IT COMES to revamping a home, most women focus on the finished product, fantasizing about sexy moldings, handsome floors, and slick appliances. They don't focus on what happens before that. In fact, most women are clueless when it comes to the actual building process. This is one of the main reasons why so many women don't have a handle on what's going on. But this doesn't have to be you.

What you need is a general overview, practical tips, and a few nuts and bolts to help you understand what's going on during the remodeling process. So now it's time for you to go behind the scenes and learn what's happening to your home.

THE THREE TRIMESTERS:
An Overview

A remodel, like a pregnancy, can be divided into trimesters. During each trimester, your home will develop in a predictable fashion, and your moods will follow along. We'll give you the details later in this chapter, but see the list that follows for the big picture.

- **The first trimester.** From the moment of inception, you will feel excited but nauseous as things start to develop:
  - Demolition
  - Foundation work
  - Framing work
  - Rough electric work and other wiring
  - Rough plumbing
  - Rough HVAC work

- **The second trimester.** This is often the easiest stage. You will be at your happiest because something is really starting to show:
  - Roofing
  - Closing exterior walls
  - Insulation
  - Closing up interior walls
  - Chimney and fireplace work
  - Subflooring

- **The third trimester.** Will this ever end? Ouch, those huge bills really hurt! The indigestion is terrible and you can't sleep. Will this "baby" be late? (It's never early.):
  - Finish flooring
  - Tile work
  - Installation of cabinetry
  - Installation of countertops
  - Finish carpentry (trim and moldings)
  - Other finish work
  - Staining
  - Painting
  - Installation of appliances and fixtures
  - Landscaping and hardscaping
  - Cleanup
  - Finishing touches

THE FIRST TRIMESTER

Finally Some Action: Demolition

Ahhh—that sweet sound of banging . . . there is a certain excitement (or, at least, a sense of relief) that you will feel when work finally begins. Beyond that feeling, though, most people do not give a lot of thought to demolition. This is a mistake. There's actually a lot to think about. There may be things you like about your home that you want to preserve—features that can be removed and put back in or left intact. And there are things you need to know about living through demolition if you are planning on living in your home during your remodel.

Living Through Demolition

Demolition is something that you probably don't want to be around for. There are potential safety issues, especially if what is being demolished involves toxic substances (for example, removal of lead paint and asbestos). Safety issues aside, the dust and noise can be nothing short of intolerable. If you are living in your home during your remodel, your contractor will need to seal off the part of the home that you'll be living in. You should store your clothes, computers, stereo equipment, computers, and anything else that could get ruined by the vast amounts of dirt and dust caused by demolition in the sealed-off area. And, any part of the home that is not being remodeled will have to be well protected, even if you are not living there while the work is being done.

If you are remodeling a house, be prepared to have an unsightly Dumpster in front of your home from the time demolition begins until the job is completed.

What Do You Want to Save?

Before demolition begins, go through your home and look around carefully. Make a list of everything you want to save. There may be things you love about your home that give it character, such as beautiful old doors, knobs, tile, or molding. Or maybe it's the light fixtures, an antique tub, or sink. Give your list to your contractor and talk to him about it. Don't rely on him to make these types of decisions for you, and don't assume that the demolition men will be careful about saving anything unless they are given very specific instructions. Think about it: It's much more difficult to have to remove something or to have to work carefully around it than it is simply to hack away. Also make sure you and your contractor agree on where you're going to store what you save; it should be somewhere safe and away from the work, dust, and debris that will be flying around.

Knocking Down or Building New Walls

With a renovation, one of the most important things for you to know is that you can't just randomly knock down walls and build new ones. When your home or building (in the case of a condo or co-op) was originally built, it was designed to withstand a variety of loads, including the materials that the home is built with, the weight of people inside, and all the things that are housed in the home (possessions and furniture). It was also designed to withstand forces such as wind or even earthquakes if you live in an earthquake zone. Certain walls provide critical support for your home and other walls do not. So, before you get excited about reconfiguring your home a certain way, you will need a contractor, structural engineer, or architect to tell you which walls can be taken down and which walls cannot. But don't get nervous if you're told that the wall you want to take down is load bearing. There may be something else you can have built to compensate for it's removal.

Another thing you will need to consider before taking down a wall is what's going on inside it. Your walls are filled with pipes, wires, and ducts that are part of your home's plumbing, electrical, heating, air-conditioning, and ventilation systems. There may also be gas lines and wires for your phones and computers or other things.

In a condo, co-op, or any other situation in which you are subject to restrictions, you may not be able to take down a wall even if it is not a structural one. For example, you may be prevented from removing a wall if there are any gas lines running through it.

Can You Really Live with It?

Every remodel is different and some lead to more inconveniences than others. For the remodeler who thought she could live through all the noise and mess and hassle, there is often a rude awakening when the work begins, and she sees what it's really like to live through it. Soon she is reevaluating her whole plan. Suddenly, she can't stand doing take-out for every meal and finds sharing a tiny bathroom with the rest of her family intolerable. She finds herself begging her husband to rent another place for their family although that was not the original plan. She knows that the added expenses will increase the budget, but this falls into the life's-too-short category of decisions.

Limitations on When It Can Be Done

Some localities and homeowners' associations (HOAs) have special regulations that deal with when demolition (as distinguished from other types of construction) can and can't be done. These regulations are designed to protect your neighbors from noise at certain times, primarily when people may be sleeping. If your property is subject to any HOA restrictions, you should know that these regulations may be different from the local building codes. Your contractor needs to honor both. Most contractors are aware of governmental building regulations but won't know about your HOA rules. It's your responsibility to find out and convey this information to him. Also, you should know that some contractors ignore these regulations altogether. It's a good idea that you make sure your contractor is going by the book if you want to avoid being hit with fines and the wrath of angry neighbors!

What You May Find After Demolition

As we've said throughout this book, no matter how vigilant you've been in planning your remodel, sometimes you never really know what you're dealing with until the walls have been opened up and floors and surfaces have been ripped out. Remember the Oh-Nos! that we talked about earlier? This is the time that many of them pop up. You may find bad plumbing pipes, unsafe wiring, termite or water damage, or structural failure. Make sure you set up a meeting with your contractor after demolition is over to reassess your project and to find out if there are any glitches.

Everything Starts with a Good Foundation: Foundation Repair and New Construction

A foundation anchors your home to the ground. It provides support and stability for the walls and roof of your home. The foundation also shields your home from elements in the ground— like water, bugs, and other things. The following sections cover what you should know about your foundation as you move forward.

Get It Checked

As we have said, before remodeling your home, it's a good idea to have your foundation checked out so you can have it repaired, if necessary. With a remodel, if you are making structural changes to your home (for example, taking down or moving walls or adding a second story), it is very important for your design and building team to learn as much about the existing foundation as possible, because what you may be removing or adding could affect it.

If You Are Rebuilding Your Home or Building an Addition

Not all foundations are built the same way. The technique used to design a foundation for your home or home addition depends on the architecture of your home itself, your site, the climate in which you live, and your budget. For things like room additions and decks, there are certain commonly used techniques that are less expensive than other methods. The more challenging your building site, the more creative your team will have to be to design a foundation that is secure. Homes built on hillsides, the ocean-front, and certain types of soil present special challenges. The more complex your foundation, the more it will cost you.

Getting into Shape: Framing

The concept of framing is really very simple. A building frame defines either an object or a space in your home. Framing is the first step to many parts of your home taking shape and developing into what it is that you'll see from the outside. The walls, floors, and roof of your home get framed. These are the larger components of your home. And then there are the details that get framed such as doors, windows, stairs, fireplaces, chimneys, and skylights. During the framing process, you may hear members of your construction team talking about things that sound like a foreign language; terms such as *floor joists* and *ceiling joists*. Refer to the Glossary so you'll know what everyone is talking about!

Once the foundation is built for a home, the next steps are to frame the floor and install any subfloor. Then the exterior walls will be erected for any part of your home that you are rebuilding and for any addition.

Don't confuse the subflooring with the finish flooring you will install in the third trimester. Subflooring is usually made of plywood. The finish flooring, such as hardwood, carpeting, tile, stone, marble, or linoleum, is installed on top of the subflooring.

Getting Rough with Utilities: Rough Plumbing, Electrical, and Other Services

At this point, any new walls that you are building have been framed and old walls that needed to be opened up are exposed. The next step is for the guys that deal with all your services to come in to install all the boxes, wires, pipes, ducts, and anything else that will need to run through the walls. These are things that you don't see once the walls are closed up, such as wiring and pipes for electricity, plumbing, HVAC, telephones, cable, computers, doorbells, smoke alarms, sound systems, and security systems.

Rough Electric Work

Electricity comes into your home from service lines that run to your property through a meter and then into a main service panel. Electrical fixtures in your home include the lighting fixtures themselves, the plugs (also called outlets or receptacles), and the switches. For each of these things, you will have a metal or plastic box in the wall, ceiling, or floor, wherever the location of the fixture, outlet, or switch. Once the walls are closed up, the fixtures, outlets, and switches are connected to the wires and attached to the box. Roughing-in an electrical system means installing the electrical boxes and running wires from the service panel to the boxes. Finished electric work requires connecting the wires and fixtures and is not done until the walls are closed up.

Rough Plumbing

You may be replacing some or all of your pipes as part of your remodel. Roughing-in the plumbing means running (or replacing) the pipes that are being worked on. Finished plumbing is the installation of the plumbing fixtures (toilets, sinks, faucets, etc.) and is usually done toward the end of your remodel.

Installation of HVAC

Before all the walls are closed up, all the ducts, pipes, or anything else your HVAC system will need that should be behind the walls, under the floors, or above the ceiling, will be installed. The thermostats, other controls, vents, and returns will be installed at a later stage of your remodel.

THE SECOND TRIMESTER

Finally, a Roof over Your Head!

If you have reduced your old home to the studs or are adding on a new addition, at this stage you will reach the mini-milestone of bringing your home under roof, which is what some builders call installing the exterior roof covering. It's a big deal because, along with installing the exterior walls onto the bare frame of the house, the completion of the exterior roof covering closes your house against the elements.

If you are adding a new roof or replacing part of your old roof, the biggest issue is your choice of roofing materials. If you are repairing the old roof, you will want to try to match the existing materials, but that is not always possible. Like any other product, roofing materials can be discontinued, and you may not be able to find an exact match. Even if you can find the same product, the old materials can become discolored with age and any new tiles will stand out. Rather than having to replace your entire roof, you can save money by getting creative. For example, you can replace visible broken tiles with old tiles from a place on your roof that isn't visible at all, or at least cannot be seen from key areas. Or you might be able to have a few tiles custom made to match the old ones. As you choose roofing materials, you will want to discuss the following considerations with your contractor:

- **Making it fireproof.** Depending on where you live, you may not be allowed by law to install anything other than fireproof roofing materials. But even if you are, you should think twice about using flammable materials like wood shakes or shingles that could easily catch on fire and put your property—and the people inside—at risk, no matter how good they look.

- **The weather report.** Some roofing materials are not appropriate in certain climates. Also, a sloping roof can be your best bet to avoid leaks or cave-ins—it won't accumulate heavy snow or water the way a flat roof does.

- **Buy quality.** Certain materials are cheaper than others, but the better the quality of the materials, the longer your roof should last. The quality of the installation work is also important.

One more thing relating to your roof are the gutters. As we said in Chapter 5, you need to make sure you have proper gutters and downspouts to collect runoff water from the roof and divert it away from your house and foundation. It is amazing how this inexpensive feature of your home can keep water away from your house and save you time and trouble in expensive repairs down the road.

Closing It All Up: Exterior Walls

Like roofing materials, the type of exterior finishes you use on your home depends not only on the style of your home but also the climate of your area.

Keeping Cool and Staying Warm: Insulation

Energy efficiency and environmental concerns have become mainstream, as people try to save energy and money on heating and cooling their homes. It doesn't matter how sophisticated your HVAC system is; it will never work at its maximum efficiency without the right insulation. But that's not the only reason to insulate; your home will always be more comfortable, even if you live in a mild climate, with the right insulation.

If your walls are opened up anyway, don't skimp on this part of your remodel. You can save a lot of money on your heating and cooling bills with insulation, and it's pretty simple—and relatively inexpensive—to do. Even if walls are not opened up, there may be accessible areas of your home (such as attic space) that could be better insulated.

Closing Up the Interior Walls: Drywall

Perhaps the most exciting step for most people during the second trimester is sealing the interior walls, and it's easy to understand why. When you walk through your home during the first trimester, try as you may, you will probably have a hard time imagining what the rooms will look like when all you can see are open walls with wires and pipes running through them. The drab color of the framing can make a room look dark. And it's hard to tell where one room starts and another ends, even though the doors and windows may already have been framed. But once the interior walls are sealed, you'll be able to visualize exactly how those rooms are going to look.

The most common material used to seal the interior walls is drywall. You've probably heard this term before, but you may not know exactly what it is. Drywall consists of large panels of plaster covered on both sides by paper. These panels are cut to fit the space as necessary to seal the walls, and are nailed or screwed right into the ceiling joists and wall studs. Drywall must be smoothed out before you can put certain types of finishes on the walls, such as paint or wallpaper, which will be done later on. The process involves taping, applying a wet material referred to as mud, which then dries and is sanded to achieve a smooth surface. But drywall does not have to be particularly smooth if you are going to install paneling, because the paneling will cover up any imperfections.

Come On, Baby, Light My Fire: Your Chimney and Fireplace

Often your chimney will be finished on the same schedule and using the same (or complementary) materials as the exterior finishes of your home. Other times, the chimney will be constructed or repaired by your chimney/fireplace subcontractor on a different schedule than the subs who are closing up the exterior walls. The fireplace might, similarly, be on a slightly different schedule from the rest of the second trimester work. The finishes (trim, mantel, etc.) will usually be completed with the other finishes during the third trimester.

THE THIRD TRIMESTER

Something You Can Walk All Over: Finished Flooring

In the second trimester, your home's subfloor was installed in any room where the flooring is being newly installed or replaced. Now it's time to install what you'll see and walk on—whether it be wood, tile, stone, carpet, or some other surface. If you're not installing new flooring but just refinishing the old (such as sanding and restaining wood floors), this is the time when the refinishing work gets done.

Depending on the type of finish flooring you are going to install, you might need to add an additional layer—called underlayment—on top of the subflooring. The purpose of the underlayment is either to support a particularly heavy flooring material or to smooth out a lack of uniformity in the subflooring that might show through a thin floor finish, such as linoleum or carpeting.

Timing Is Key

When exactly flooring should be finished is often a big question. If the finish is carpeting, the answer is easy; it will almost always be installed at the tail end of the project. But for other types of flooring, whether it's done before or after painting is often one of the biggest questions. There are a few issues to consider. First, while the

Don't Waste Your Money

If you know for sure that you are going to put wall-to-wall carpeting in a room, don't bother spending lots of money on finish flooring. Just put down a plywood subfloor or concrete slab and call it a day—no one will see it.

floors are being done, no one else can work in that area, so all other work going on in that room will be on hold until the floors are completed. Second, out of everything in the home, floors get the most wear and tear. While nothing stays perfect forever, both you and your contractor will want everything to be as close to perfect as possible when your remodel is done. Discuss with your contractor what he thinks would be best, paying particular attention to how best to protect the floors and the rest of the work to be done. He may recommend different things for different rooms. For example, if you are putting tile down in a bathroom and installing hardwood in the living room, he may recommend that the tile be laid at the same time that the hardwood is installed but that the hardwood not be stained and finished until almost everything else in the house is done. If you are both painting the walls and refinishing hardwood in a particular room, most contractors will sand down the wood first (a horribly dusty process), then clean and paint the walls, and, finally, stain and finish the floors.

Different Types of Flooring

- **Hardwood.** Wood flooring is one of the most popular and expensive types of flooring. It is particularly popular for common areas such as living and dining rooms, and for some people it is the way to go for most of the home. The downside to hardwood is that it scratches easily (some types of wood scratch more easily than others) and is not as durable or water resistant as other materials such as tile. One flood from a broken pipe or a sink that overflows and a gorgeous and expensive floor can quickly warp and, effectively, be destroyed. This is why many people would never consider using it in areas such as bathrooms or kitchens. On the other hand, some of the hottest kitchen and bathroom designs feature hardwood flooring, and you may decide that you have to have it in these rooms even if it's not the most practical.

- **Composite floors**. If you like the look of wood but can't afford it, there are substitutes that are much less expensive. These are composite materials onto which a material that looks like wood is laminated.

- **Tile**. Tile is also one of the more commonly used flooring materials and there is a huge variety to choose from, including ceramic and stone tile, and tile made from other natural materials. The range in price is also huge. There are types of tile that are very durable and can be cleaned easily and other types of tile that may be impractical to use as flooring material (such as hand-painted tile, which may not stand up to all the wear and tear and cleaning that floors typically demand). Also, certain types of materials are very slippery especially when wet (such as tile made of polished marble). This is an important thing to consider when you are choosing your flooring materials. If you are buying your own tile, always make sure to buy a little more than you are told you'll need in case some break during installation or you need to fix tiles that break down the road. You'll want to make sure everything matches and, if you don't have any spare tile, you risk the next lot varying a bit in color or even the possibility that it isn't made anymore.

- **Other flooring materials**. There are other flooring materials you might consider. Linoleum has made a comeback with new and improved designs, colors, and textures. Good linoleum is generally durable and can cost less than other flooring materials. Concrete floors have become popular in homes with modern decor, and it's amazing what can be done with tinting and texture of concrete. Concrete can even be made to look like stone and is now sometimes also used for fireplace mantels and countertops. Contrary to what you might think, interior concrete flooring is usually very expensive.

Tiling Beyond the Floors

Tile is used to cover many other surfaces besides floors; walls and showers in bathrooms frequently get tiled as do backsplashes in kitchens and laundry rooms. Countertops in kitchens, bathrooms, and laundry rooms are also commonly tiled. If you are tiling a bathroom wall or ceiling, the tile work will be done before any walls are painted. If you are tiling a kitchen countertop and/or kitchen backsplash, this will be done after the cabinets are put in.

Size and Shape

Generally, larger tiles are used for flooring and smaller tiles used for everything else, but there is no hard-and-fast rule. Depending on what type of surface you are tiling, you may very well need to order *trim tile*, which is tile shaped to finish off corners and edges such as countertop surfaces, in addition to the main tile, which is called the *field tile*. Trim tile comes in different shapes, and there are names for each (for example, bullnose tile). If you are shopping for tile yourself, make sure you find out from your contractor or tile guy if you need trim tile and, if you do, what shape you'll need and if it's available to match or coordinate with your field tile.

Inspect Everything First

*A*s soon as something you've ordered arrives at your home, unwrap it and check it out right away. You want to inspect it for any flaws, damage, or breakage that occurred in manufacturing or shipping. For example, tile can arrive broken, prefinished cabinets could come with flaws, and the shipper may even have sent you the wrong thing. You should look at everything immediately so you'll know that it was the manufacturer or shipper, and not the contractor or someone else on site, who did any damage. You'll also want to have enough time to send anything back that needs to be replaced. (Remember, replacements might not always be in stock or might take a long time to ship.) Once your delivery checks out, then you'll want to store it carefully and in a safe place, as you and your contractor should have agreed.

Choose Your Own Grout

Another design choice you'll be making if you are using tile is the color of your grout. Grout is what seals the joints (or spaces) between the tiles. Many people pay little or no attention to the grout color but this subtle detail can make a difference. The closer the grout color is to the tile, the less busy (and some would say more formal) the surface looks. By contrast, the more the grout contrasts with the tile, the busier the surface will look.

Storing All Your Stuff: Cabinetry

If you are putting down new floors, cabinets and built-ins may be installed before or after the finished flooring. Talk to your contractor about what he recommends. In a kitchen, which typically has both upper and lower cabinets, the upper cabinets will almost always be installed first since it's much easier to hang them without the interference of the lower cabinets.

Type and Finish

Cabinets can be custom made or prefabricated. If you are having a cabinetmaker build any of your cabinets, they may be stained or painted off site or they may be finished at your home after being installed. Most prebuilt cabinets are delivered already finished (stained or painted), and it can be difficult to touch up any scratches or marks. Make sure they are being stored in a safe place well protected until it's time for installation.

Getting the Fit Just Right

Cabinetry, especially for kitchens, is one of those things that must be meticulously planned out down to the last inch. So, as we told you in previous chapters, a kitchen designer or space planner could really come in handy when it comes to configuring your cabinetry.

Over the Counter: Countertops

After the cabinet installation comes the installation of the countertops. We have already talked a little about tile countertops and the importance of making sure you have the right trim tile. There are a few other things you should know about countertops. In addition to tile, common choices for countertops are stone such as granite, marble, slate, limestone and bluestone; plastic laminates such as Formica; synthetic stone such as Corian; stainless steel (usually just for kitchens); and wood. Granite is one of the most durable materials, and it is also one of the most expensive. It is heat resistant, scratch resistant, and typically does not stain easily. Granite is a great choice for kitchens. Wood (such as butcher block), on the other hand, may look beautiful but it scratches and can be scorched easily. It can also be easily damaged by water.

A big issue with countertops is the design of the edge. The more elaborate the design, the more expensive the countertop is likely to be. Also, remember that, for any area where you need to insert a fixture (such as your sink) into the countertop, there will be an additional charge for labor for the cutout of the countertop where the fixture goes.

Details, Details: Trim and Molding

Trim covers the seams of construction. Trim is applied around the edges of windows and doors to cover the frames. It also covers the edges between the flooring and the walls. Special trim (also called molding) such as wainscoting, crown molding, and baseboards decorates walls and adds detail and character to a room. Trim can be made of inexpensive composite materials, less expensive wood, or expensive exotic wood.

Finishing Your Trim

*K*eep in mind that painting or staining trim is a painstaking job. The more trim you have in your home (think doors, windows, and moldings), and the more elaborate your trim is, the more it'll cost you.

Finally Some Color: Painting

Like changing your hairstyle when you're bored with your look, painting can be one of the least expensive ways to give your home a makeover. On the other hand, it may cost more than you think. "What's the big deal about slapping some coats of paint on a wall?" you may ask. There's a lot more that goes into a good paint job than you may know. Preparing surfaces before painting is key if the finish is going to last. Whether it's an interior or exterior paint job, a painter has to deal with any moisture problems that may be apparent, scrape free all existing paint that is chipping or cracked, fill and sand all irregularities, and prime the surfaces. Having to strip and patch an existing wall that has already been painted and is showing its age is more work than painting a brand-new wall.

Choosing Your Paint

There are three main things to consider when choosing your paint: where it's going, finish, and color.

- **Indoors or outdoors?** Paint that is designed for application on your home's exterior is made to stand up to the elements in a way that interior paint is not. (Remember, you may need to get approval for the color you want to paint the exterior of your home from your homeowners' association if you live in a planned community.)

- **Finish**. Paint comes in various sheens—from flat to semigloss (also commonly known as eggshell) to glossy. Flat paint gives a soft, flat finish; and many people like how it looks better than a paint that has some sheen to it. The problem with flat paint is that it's hard to clean. You may rub off some paint in the process of trying to rub off a stain. The more sheen to the paint, the easier it is to keep clean and the more water resistant it tends to be. A glossy or semigloss paint is ideal for things that get touched a lot or are exposed to moisture, such as bathrooms, window trim, moldings, and doors. For those who prefer the look of a flatter finish but need to be practical, an eggshell finish is often a good compromise for rooms in which the walls are likely to get dirty, such as kids' rooms, playrooms, kitchens, bathrooms, and laundry rooms.

- **Color.** Choosing paint colors is one of the most fun parts of remodeling. With color, you can completely change the mood of a room. Whether you are working with an interior designer or not, there are a few things to keep in mind. Don't just focus on one room at a time. Keep in mind the flow of the home from one room to another. Also, you may love the color you see on someone else's wall, on a paint swatch at the paint store, or even on a paint swatch that you hold up in the room you are painting, but you may detest it when it goes up on the walls. Or, less dramatically, you may not hate it but it may not look quite right. The color on a paint swatch may be different from the paint you actually get in the can. In addition to how the paint is mixed, there are many other things that influence how the color looks, including the other colors in the room such as the color of the ceiling, trim, and molding; the color of other things you will have in the room such as furniture; the color of the floors; and the quality of the light in the room. Colors will look different in artificial and natural light, and will look different in the morning, during the afternoon, and at night. The best way to get a handle on what the color will look like and whether you like it is to paint a large portion of a wall or two in the room you are

Sample Sales

It's sometimes hard to find just the right color. We know women who have gone through over one hundred paint samples in choosing the paint colors for their homes. Paint is usually sold by the gallon or quart—using lots of gallons or even quarts for samples can really add up! But you don't necessarily have to spend that much—some paint manufacturers will sell much smaller amounts specifically for sampling.

painting (a small little patch won't cut it) and look at it in all kinds of light.

Sometimes It's All About Brands

Some painters prefer using a specific brand because they are used to it; they are familiar with the color and finishes and the store may be convenient for them. You may have another brand that you want to use based on conversations with friends or your designer. We have found that some brands clean better than others and that the sheen may vary brand to brand. An eggshell finish from one company may look more or less shiny than that from another. One brand's flat paint may clean better than another. Make sure you specify with your contractor and painters which brand you want to use. Buying good-quality paint does make a difference.

Special Techniques

Specialty finishes such as Venetian plaster and textured walls require more talent than the standard paint job. Some painters are more like artists and can do just about any type of finish you want. In other cases, you may have to hire someone besides your main painter.

Can You Live in the House While Painting Is Going On?

Painting is a very smelly process and it's not pleasant breathing the fumes. However, there are things that can be done to reduce the smell such as sealing off the part of the house that is being painted and keeping doors and windows to the outside open. It really depends on how much of your home you are painting at once and the type of paint you use. Oil-based paint smells worse than water-based paint, and it takes longer for the smell to go away.

After It's All Done

After the paint is on the walls, you can really see what a room looks like and you will feel like you have reached a huge milestone in your remodel. Finally, the light is shining brightly at the end of the tunnel!

Here Come the Appliances and Fixtures!

We covered buying your appliances earlier. Their installation is often one of the last steps in remodeling. Generally speaking, this goes pretty quickly, and within one or two days you can go from having no functioning kitchen at all to having the kitchen of your dreams.

Who Does the Work?

New bathroom and electric fixtures will be installed by your contractor's crew, but your contractor will not necessarily be doing the work or using his guys to install appliances. Frequently, they are installed by the store where you bought them or by a contractor or company that specializes in installing appliances.

The Great Outdoors: Landscaping and Hardscaping

Landscaping and hardscaping are usually done at the end of the renovation, generally to avoid that beautiful lawn being trampled by workers and that newly paved driveway being ruined by heavy trucks and equipment. If you have not been living in your home during the renovation, you do not have to finish the outdoors to be able to use the home.

Cleaning Up the Mess

As we noted earlier, it is a good idea to have a clause in your contract with your contractor requiring him to clean up the place when he's done. Although most contractors will leave the place broom clean, this doesn't mean you'll find the place livable. You'll still need to get rid of all the dust, dirt, and grime as well as stray nails, screws, and other dangerous building materials that his guys inadvertently missed. But this is no job for your regular cleaning lady—especially if you want her to come back! Instead, consider hiring a professional service that specializes in cleaning up homes after construction to really get the place spic-and-span.

The Finishing Touches

You're almost done! The last step to completing your remodel is to install any wall coverings and carpeting, as well as light fixtures and little things like towel bars, knobs, and toilet-paper holders. You thought this day would never come . . . after all the dust and drama, chaos and disruption, the fun and the fights, your contractor is finally finished. He and his subcontractors are finally going to leave. Or are they . . . ?

PART 4

Finishing Up

The Punch List Means Never Having to Say Good-Bye:
GETTING YOUR CONTRACTOR TO FINISH THE WORK

AFTER YOUR CONTRACTOR says he's finished, after the final inspection, and even after you can start using your newly remodeled space, it's still not quite over! You and your contractor should count on seeing each other for a bit longer. That's because there are probably odds and ends that still require his attention, which you will discover when you walk through your home and make your punch list. So, although your contractor will probably ask you for final payment at this point, don't get your checkbook out just yet. Remember, you should never pay your contractor the final payment until he has completed all the items on the punch list.

HANGING IN THERE TILL THE END

This time can be trying for both you and your contractor. You know how tired you are of seeing each other. You won't be talking as often, and finishing up the little things

Punch List Recap

It's usually about the little things: missing knobs, broken tiles, missing switch plates, and paint touch-ups, for example. But larger things—particularly if they are repairs—may also be an issue.

may seem to take forever. You are not his main squeeze anymore. His thoughts (and his subcontractors') are probably already committed to a new project. And if things have gotten tense between the two of you, he might just disappear. This is why you must make sure you are holding enough money for the final payment to make it worth his while to finish your job.

The strange thing is, sometimes it's hard to persuade even the most conscientious contractor to finish your punch list. In fact, sometimes no amount of money is enough incentive if he is too disorganized or too distracted by other work to get back to finish your project. Sometimes you'll have to use that final payment you're holding to hire someone else to finish up what your contractor didn't. Consider Ellen's experience at the end of her remodel.

> *Ellen and Steve had a good experience working with Dan, their contractor, when they converted their detached garage into an office. After most of the work was done and they got their final permit, they noticed that there were a few things that Dan hadn't done. The gutters still hadn't been installed on the outside of the structure, the cabinets had no knobs, and there were problems with some of the electrical outlets. Even though they were still holding the last $15,000 that was due to Dan, Steve and Ellen couldn't get him to return their phone calls, let alone come over to their house to finish the work. It was as though he had vanished. After three months of trying again and again to reach Dan, they gave up. They ended up using the money they were holding to hire another contractor to finish up. They never heard from Dan again.*

Each contract and set of circumstances is different, so if you find yourself in the position of holding money because your contractor

hasn't completed the work, it's a good idea to run the situation by an
attorney before you hire and pay another contractor to finish the job.

THE EVER-GROWING PUNCH LIST

Even after you've made your initial punch list, expect it to grow
once you've been living in your remodeled space for a while. Be on
the lookout for things that are broken, weren't finished, or weren't
installed properly. These are things that the final walk-through
might not have revealed. There are some things you simply won't
notice unless you are living there. For example, you won't discover that the toilet doesn't flush properly until you start using it. You
won't know that the hot and cold knobs on your bathtub have
been reversed until you stick your toe into a tub of freezing cold
water. Or that faulty window installation may come to light only
when you notice a draft coming into your bedroom at night.

Don't get too comfortable with these little imperfections. It's easy
to overlook minor flaws and just get used to living with them. As we
pointed out before, you probably got used to living with your home's
quirks before you remodeled. Don't do this again! Make a list of
things that are wrong and get your contractor to fix everything.

16

Moving Madness:
MOVING IN . . .
OR MOVING BACK IN

AT LONG LAST, it's time to move in. If your project was relatively small and you lived in your home throughout, you'll really be settling in rather than moving in. But if you're first moving in or you're moving back, there are lots of things you need to take care of.

GETTING EVERYTHING AND EVERYBODY READY

The first rule of moving is to be organized. And remember, you not only will be preparing yourself and your old household for the move but will also be prepping your new home for your arrival.

Your home has been a construction site for a while and you'll need to get the place cleaned up. Make sure your contractor or cleaning crew has cleared all debris and dangerous materials from both the inside and outside. You don't want to get a flat tire from stray nails, and you certainly don't want anyone stepping on them!

Don't forget that your home needs to be as fully functional as possible before you move in. Make sure your utilities are hooked up. Cable or satellite TV might not be a necessity before you move in, but phone, water, heat, gas and electricity certainly are, and few people can live without Internet access these days.

THE MOVING MEN

You may have moved many times in your life. All you needed when you moved into your first place was one Saturday, a few strong friends, a dolly, and your cousin's boyfriend's pickup truck or SUV. Smile at those happy memories but don't get caught up in the nostalgia. You are most likely no longer at the stage in your life when you should be considering having anyone other than professional, insured, and bonded movers to do the job for you, no matter how much money you think you could save. It will not be worth the time, aggravation, broken belongings, or sore muscles—not to mention the dings to the freshly painted walls in your beautifully remodeled home. Do everyone a favor and hire reputable movers.

Pack It Yourself or Hire Packers?

With the huge expenses of remodeling and moving, you might be tempted to pack your own boxes. This might be easy if you are moving things out of and back into a few rooms. But when you are packing up and moving an entire household from one place to another, consider having your professional movers pack up the place for you. They can almost certainly pack breakables, disassemble furniture, and unplug and pack electronic devices much better than you can. Plus, they'll be faster than you can be—not only because it's their job but also because they won't linger over every last vase, candle, or photograph, reliving all those memories the way you would.

Hiring movers is just like hiring a contractor—there are good ones and bad ones. Your goal is to hire professional movers who will make moving day as effortless for you as possible, take good care of your stuff in transport, and not damage your beautifully remodeled home. Ask your friends, neighbors, and coworkers for referrals, and ask questions about their experiences. Make sure whomever you hire has adequate insurance. And don't forget to book well in advance—good movers, like good contractors, get busy.

PARTING WAYS WITH SOME OF YOUR THINGS

Anytime you remodel, it's a great opportunity to clean out your drawers, closets, cabinets, and shelves. There are probably many things that you'll never use again, like that box of who-knows-what that no doubt will try to sneak its way into a corner of your new garage like it did in your old one! We recommend that you divide your belongings into three categories, regardless of whether you are packing your own boxes or hiring your movers to do it: the must-haves, the maybes, and the absolutely-nos. Help the absolutely-nos find their way to your local charity or a yard sale. Bring the must-haves and maybes with you . . . you can deal with them later.

MOVING DAY

Moving day is always more exhausting and overwhelming than you think it will be. One way to make it a little easier on yourself is to think ahead. Here are some useful tips:

- Be present when the movers load up at your old place to make sure everything gets on the truck. You'd be surprised at how often things get left behind.

- Be at the new place when the movers show up—they'll need you to show them where to put things. And you'll certainly want to make sure they are protecting your remodeled home from damage. For example, you'll want to make sure they cover things that can get scratched like new hardwood floors.

- Pack an overnight bag for you and each member of your family as though you were planning a weekend away, complete with several changes of clothes, pajamas, and all your toiletries and beauty products. The day you move and the few days after are not the time to try to find your shampoo or work clothes in a sea of boxes!

- Make sure you have basic provisions—a roll of toilet paper, paper towels, bath towels, a carton of milk, or anything else you may need. Buy these things ahead of time—the last thing you'll want to do at the end of the day when you're ready to collapse is to have to head to the store to buy them.

- Consider leaving your small children with relatives or friends for the day. You don't need the added stress of trying to calm or entertain bored children . . . or of trying to keep them safe. But if this isn't possible, make sure you have plenty of toys to keep them occupied and provisions to keep them fed and happy.

- Consider boarding your pets while you pack and move. You also don't need your cat or dog to get lost in the commotion and chaos of moving day.

- It's easy to get all excited on moving day and forget to eat. Make sure you have plenty of drinks and snacks available. You'll need the energy, and if you don't eat, you'll get really cranky.

- Make sure you have those bed linens ready and that your movers set up your bed so you can fall right into it—you can start unpacking your first box tomorrow.

Afterword
THE REMODELING QUEEN AND HER EVER-CHANGING CASTLE

You already know that construction does not end suddenly—it's not like one day your house is filled with dust, debris, and workmen, and the next day everyone has vanished in a puff of smoke to reveal perfection. Things drag on even after you start unpacking boxes.

But then one day you realize that you haven't answered the door in your bathrobe for a while. And while you would think that you'd be happy to have life get back to normal, at the same time, you might feel like something is missing. The quiet and lack of chaos might start to get to you, and you may start feeling wistful and nostalgic for those days when you were running to the paint store three times a week and something new and exciting was going on in your house every day. You start to forget about the aggravation, and start thinking about what changes you are going to make next. Now you know what to do . . . on to your next project!

Resources

FINDING GENERAL CONTRACTORS

Angie's List: *www.angieslist.com*. Members joining after paying a fee can use this consumer network to find contractors in a host of trades in one of more than seventy cities across the United States. Members themselves rate their experiences with contractors, and the ratings are posted on the site.

GoPro.ca: *www.gopro.ca* (Canada only). A listing of various contractors and service providers across Canada.

PROFESSIONAL ORGANIZATIONS

National Association of the Remodeling Industry (NARI): *www.nari.org*. A national trade association of contractors that certifies its members through screening and testing; the website offers assistance to homeowners in finding member contractors.

National Institute of Building Inspectors (NIBI): *www.nibi.com.* An association that trains and certifies home inspectors. The website offers assistance in finding NIBI-certified home inspectors in the United States and Canada.

American Institute of Architects (AIA): *www.aia.org.* A national professional association of architects. The website offers assistance in finding AIA member architects.

American Society of Interior Designers, Inc. (ASID): *www.asid.org.* A national professional association of interior designers. The website offers assistance in finding member designers.

American Society of Landscape Architects (ASLA): *www.asla.org.* A national professional association of landscape architects; the website describes the profession. The website offers assistance in finding member landscape architects.

National Kitchen & Bath Association (NKBA): *www.nkba.org.* A national professional association of kitchen and bath specialists; the website offers consumer assistance and advice on planning a kitchen or bath remodel, including an online remodeling guide and assistance in finding member professionals.

CONTRACTORS:
Licensing, Lawsuits, and Insurance

Abika: *www.abika.com/reports/professionallicenses.htm.* (For the United States and Canada.) For a fee, you can get information about the status of a contractor's license; status of his insurance; any lawsuits filed against him; and general liens, judgments and bankruptcy filings as well as a twenty-year address history.

Better Business Bureau: *www.bbb.org.* Locate Better Business Bureaus across the United States and Canada. You can get information about whether a contractor has the required state licenses, whether any consumer complaints have been filed against him and the status of any such complaint. If you cannot find this information on the website, contact your local BBB office.

State attorneys general offices: *www.statelocalgov.net/50statesattorney-general.cfm*. A state-by-state list of attorneys general offices, located throughout the United States, with phone numbers and links to their websites. They have information about lawsuits filed against any contractor and the status of such lawsuits. They may also provide information about whether the contractor has the required licenses.

INFORMATION ABOUT MOLD, ASBESTOS, AND LEAD

Centers for Disease Control and Prevention: *www.cdc.gov*. Because the Centers for Disease Control and Prevention is a key U.S. agency responsible for public health, you'll find information about household hazards on this website that are considered dangerous to public health.

U.S. Environmental Protection Agency: *www.epa.gov*. The EPA website is a good place to start when researching any hazardous substance that you might find in your home or bring into your home during your remodel.

COST VERSUS VALUE REPORTS AND TRENDS

Remodeling Online: *www.remodeling.hw.net*. Go into the "cost versus value" link in the "special features" section for a comparison of construction costs for common remodeling projects with the value they added at resale in sixty major U.S. housing markets. Also, under the "search" option, type in keyword "trends" for various articles about what is popular.

CHILD PROOFING

U.S. Consumer Product Safety Commission:
www.cpsc.gov/cpscpub/grand/12steps/12steps.html. This site provides information about twelve safety devices to protect your children in the home.

Home Contractors.Biz: *www.homecontractros.biz.* Find child-proofing services in your area.

REMODEL THIS!

Remodel This! *www.remodelthis.net.* If you liked our book, you'll love visiting our website!

Glossary

YOU MAY NOT be doing the heavy lifting during your remodel, but you still want to be able to talk the talk. Here are some terms you may run into.

ALLOWANCES: The projected cost for the labor and/or materials for a portion of your project for which the cost has not yet been determined. Often noted as a line item in the bid or an amount designated in a construction contract.

AMPERES (AMPS): A standard measure of the rate at which electrical current (that is, the juice running through your wires) flows.

APPRAISAL: A professional estimate of the value of a piece of property, such as your home. For a remodel, you are most likely to need an appraisal of your home if you are getting a loan to pay for the work that will be secured by a mortgage.

ARBITRATION: A formal proceeding for resolving disputes in front of an impartial third party (often an attorney or retired judge) that does not involve going to court.

ASBESTOS: A building material once widely used in insulation due to its fire-resistant properties; now banned because of its connection to lung cancer and other lung disease. Often found in older homes and often must be removed.

BACKFILL: Filling in around the home's foundation; also the earth that is used to fill in around the foundation.

BACKSPLASH: A protective panel made of ceramic tile, stone, or other materials. A backsplash is installed on a wall perpendicular to a sink, stove, or counter. It not only protects the wall from water and stains but also can be a key decorative element. Usually found in kitchens, bathrooms, and laundry rooms.

BALUSTERS: Vertical members of a stair rail.

BALUSTRADE: Stair rail including handrail, posts, and balusters.

BASEBOARD: A finish board used to cover joints at the intersection of the wall and floor.

BAY OR BOW WINDOW: A window that projects outside of the exterior wall of the home.

BEADBOARD: A type of paneling that has strips of wood separated by an indentation called a bead. Often used for wainscoting.

BEAM: A piece of wood or steel used to support the weight of the floor or ceiling joist or other load.

BEARING WALL: A wall that supports part of the structure; also called a load-bearing or structural wall. This type of wall can't be easily taken down or moved unless and until another support system is built to compensate for its removal.

BID: A written statement from a contractor specifying how much he will charge to do the described construction work.

BLUEPRINTS: Working plans prepared by an architect or designer. So called because they used to be either printed with blue ink on a white background or white ink on a blue background. These days, blueprints can be in black and white.

BUILDER-GRADE MATERIALS: Products, like windows or doors, of average quality and reasonable price.

BUILDING CODES: National, state, and local regulations of construction and building techniques, materials, and occupancy; primarily address public health and safety concerns.

BUILDING DEPARTMENT: The governmental office typically responsible for approving building plans, issuing building permits, and enforcing building codes.

BUILDING PERMIT: Official authorization or permission issued by a local governmental authority for construction or renovation.

BULLNOSE: A type of trim tile used for the top part of wainscoting, for finishing bath or kitchen countertops, or for turning a corner.

CANTILEVER: A part of a structure (such as a deck) that projects beyond the main support system, such as the ground. Must be balanced by vertical support.

CASEMENT WINDOW: A window with a sash that opens inward or outward from a vertical edge.

CASING: Molding or trim around a window or door.

CAULK: A waterproof, putty-like material used to seal cracks and seams.

CEILING JOISTS: Part of the home's framing that supports the ceiling.

CERTIFICATE OF OCCUPANCY (C OF O): A document permitting legal habitation of a building issued by the local governmental authority. Temporary C of Os are often issued during construction if the issuing authority determines that the property is habitable. Final C of Os are usually issued in connection with the final sign-off on building permits once building code requirements have been met.

CHAIR RAIL: A decorative molding that runs horizontally along a wall, often about three feet from the floor (that is, chair height), but it could be at a different height. Often used to cap the top of wainscoting.

CHANGE ORDER: A written modification of a construction contract between contractor and homeowner changing some aspect of the work; a change order should detail the materials, labor, and costs of the modified work.

CIRCUIT BREAKERS: Switches located in the electrical service panel or circuit breaker box that shut down power to a portion of the home and limit the amount of power flowing through the circuit. Make sure your electrician labels each circuit breaker so you will know which one controls the flow of electricity to which part of your home.

CLAPBOARD: Siding made up of horizontal wooden boards.

CODES: See *Building codes*.

COLLATERAL: Something of value used to secure a loan. Your home can be used as collateral to secure a loan you obtain to finance your remodel.

COMPLETION BOND: A guaranty from an insurer to pay the additional money needed to complete a construction project as specified in a construction contract should the work in the contract not be completed by the contractor.

CONDUIT: A tube used to enclose wire or cables, made of metal, fiber, or plastic.

CONSTRUCTION DOCUMENTS: Detailed drawings and specifications prepared by an architect containing enough detail from which the contractor can build.

CONTINGENCY: An amount of money built into your construction budget to cover the unexpected, often noted as a line item in the bid or an amount designated in a construction contract.

COST ESTIMATE: A rough projection of the potential costs of a remodel based on rough plans or ideas, often obtained several times, at different stages of planning, so that the homeowner can develop the scope and budget of the project. A cost estimate is not a commitment from the contractor to do the work for the amount in the estimate.

COST-PLUS CONSTRUCTION CONTRACT: A contract in which the contract price is not set but is stated as the actual cost for labor, materials, and equipment provided by the contractor, plus a markup for his overhead and profit. Usually, these costs are determined as the project goes along.

CRAWL SPACE: A shallow space below a house that has no basement, located between the first-story floor joists and the ground.

CROWN MOLDING: A molding installed at the place in a room where the ceiling and the top of the wall meet. Often used as a decorative element in a room.

DOUBLE-HUNG WINDOW: A window with two sashes hung vertically that each slide independently and past each other.

DORMER: A structure that projects from a slanted roof to form another roofed area.

DOWNSPOUT: A pipe that allows water to drain from roof gutters.

DRY ROT: The fungal damage to or destruction of wood caused by excess moisture. Often disclosed by a termite or pest inspection.

DRYWALL: Panels of plaster covered on both sides by paper used to cover the framing of interior walls and ceilings.

DUMPSTER: Brand of large metal container used on construction sites to hold construction debris and rubbish.

EAVES: The lower edge of the roof projecting beyond the face of the walls.

ELEVATIONS: Drawings of interior and exterior walls used to show various details and finish features.

EQUITY: The value of a home, less the total debt on it.

ESTIMATE: An approximation of construction costs; distinguish from a bid.

FACADE: The outside face of a building.

FINAL COMPLETION: The point at which construction is fully finished, including the punch list, and no further work remains to be done. Do not confuse with *Substantial completion*.

FINISH CARPENTRY: The detailed carpentry work, such as that done for doors, windows, stairways, and moldings, needed to complete the interior of the home.

FINISH ELECTRICAL WORK: The installation of the visible parts of the electrical system, such as the fixtures, plugs, switches, and switch plates.

FINISH PLUMBING: The installation of the plumbing fixtures, faucets, and other visible parts of the plumbing system.

FITTING: In plumbing, any device that connects pipe to pipe or pipe to fixture.

FIXED-PRICE CONTRACT: A construction contract in which the contractor agrees to complete the project for a set price.

FIXTURE: The visible parts of the plumbing or electrical system attached to the floors, ceilings, or walls of the home, such as toilets, sinks, wall sconces, or ceiling lights.

FLASHING: A material (often metal) used at the intersection of different surfaces (such as the point at which the roof meets the top of an exterior wall) used to prevent the entry of water.

FLOOR JOISTS: Part of the home's framing that supports the floor.

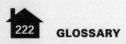

FLOOR PLAN: An architectural drawing showing the location of rooms in the home, as seen from above.

FOOTING: The base that supports a foundation wall, pier, or other type of structural wall, usually made wider than the object it supports.

FOUNDATION: The supporting portion of the structure below the first-floor or below grade.

FRAMING: The skeleton of the building underneath the interior and exterior wall coverings and roof; also the enclosing woodwork around the doors and windows.

FUSE: An electrical safety device that interrupts the flow of electrical current when it gets too high.

GALVANIZED STEEL PIPES: Plumbing pipes commonly found in older construction. Copper piping is considered superior and is often used now in place of galvanized steel.

GIRDER: A heavy beam used to support part of the structure above it, such as walls and floor joists.

GRADE: The ground level surrounding the home.

GROUND FAULT INTERRUPTER (GFI): A type of electrical outlet used near water; it protects against electric shock by automatically shutting off when detecting a short circuit.

GROUT: A substance used to fill joints and cavities in masonry work and other types of tile work. In homes, it is commonly used to fill in the spaces between ceramic or stone tile and is colored to match or contrast with the tile. (If you are doing tile work, you'll need to pick the color of your grout.)

GUTTER: A channel on a roof that catches and directs rainwater from the roof to downspouts so that water does not collect on the roof and cause damage.

HVAC: Abbreviation for heating, ventilation and air-conditioning system.

JAMB: The frame (sides and tops) of a window or door.

JOISTS: Beams used to support the weight of the floor and ceiling. Joists are supported by larger beams, girders, or load-bearing walls. See *Ceiling joists* and *Floor joists.*

KICK PLATE: A metal plate or strip that runs along the bottom edge of a door to protect the finish.

LATH OR LATHE: Material that acts as the backing for plaster or stucco.

LIABILITY INSURANCE: A type of insurance carried by a contractor or homeowner insuring against a claim by a third party against the insured for injury to people or damage to property.

LIGHT: An individual pane of glass or opening for a pane of glass in a window or door. A window or door is often described by how many lights it contains.

MASONRY: The construction of brick, stone, concrete, or other material.

MECHANIC'S LIEN: An encumbrance placed on the home by a contractor, subcontractor, supplier, or other party entitled to payment on the construction work. Filed to secure payment for unpaid bills.

MECHANIC'S LIEN WAIVER: A formal document signed by a contractor, subcontractor, supplier, or other party entitled to file a mechanic's lien waiving the right to file such a lien. Typically given in exchange for payment of a bill for the project.

MEDIATION: A nonbinding, voluntary, and informal form of dispute resolution before an impartial mediator. If a dispute cannot be resolved by mediation, then the parties may initiate arbitration or court proceedings.

MOLDING: An ornamental panel or piece of wood or other material, typically used for finishing, decoration, and/or to cover an area where two surfaces meet, such as the space between walls and ceilings or around door and window openings.

MUD: A wet material applied to drywall that then dries and gets sanded in order to create a smooth surface. See also *Spackle*.

NONBEARING WALL: A nonstructural, non-load-bearing wall.

OVERHANG: The part of a roof that projects beyond a wall.

PARTICLEBOARD: An inexpensive alternative to plywood.

PIER: A column that can be used to support various structural elements of the home, such as foundations and decks.

PLYWOOD: A wood building product used in construction made up of layers of wood veneer bonded together with adhesive.

PROGRESS PAYMENT: One of the periodic payments made to the contractor as construction work progresses.

PUNCH LIST: A written list of unfinished or incorrectly completed items that must be finished or corrected. The punch list items should be completed before final payment to the general contractor.

REBAR: Abbreviation for reinforcing bar; metal bar used to reinforce concrete.

RETAINAGE: The amount held back by an owner from each progress payment to a contractor as security that the work will be finished, paid at the end of the project on final completion.

ROUGH-IN: The preliminary installation of your home's systems during the framing stage, done before the walls are closed up. (You may hear the terms "rough plumbing" or "rough electric," for example.)

SASH: The operable or moving part of the frame of the window.

SCHEMATIC DESIGNS: Preliminary drawings prepared by architects.

SCRATCH COAT: The first of three coats of plaster.

SEPTIC TANK: A holding tank that is part of a private sewage system.

SERVICE PANEL: The metal box into which the main electrical service cable is connected and from which the house wiring is routed through circuit breakers or fuses.

SETBACK: The minimum distance between structures and property lines required by zoning or other legal requirements.

SHAKE: A type of wood shingle.

SIDING: The finish layer that covers exterior walls.

SLAB: A concrete foundation poured directly onto the ground. It is more difficult to do work underneath a home or part of a home that sits on a slab, as opposed to a home that has a crawl space or a basement.

SOFFIT: The underside portion of an overhang.

SPACKLE: A brand of quick-drying plasterlike material used for patching; plasterwork; to patch with Spackle.

SPECIFICATIONS: Written or printed construction details describing exactly what will be done and what materials will be used.

STUDS: A series of wood or metal framing beams that run vertically and provide support for walls and partitions.

SUBFLOOR: Wood boards made of plywood or particleboard laid over and attached to the foundation. The finished floor is installed on top of the subfloor.

SUBPANEL: A secondary electrical service panel installed to serve a specific area (or zone) of the home.

SUBSTANTIAL COMPLETION: The point at which construction has been completed such that the room or home can be used, but some work still needs to be done. The final governmental inspections and sign-offs may not yet have occurred and the punch list items may not have been completed.

TIME-AND-MATERIALS ARRANGEMENT: When a contractor charges for his work at an hourly rate, plus the cost of materials.

TONGUE AND GROOVE: Wood that has been cut so that the edge of one board (the tongue) fits into the grooved edge of another board. Often used for flooring and ceilings.

UNDERLAYMENT: Material placed on a subfloor if needed to provide a smooth surface for certain types of finished flooring.

VARIANCE: An exception to a zoning rule or ordinance granted by a local zoning board or other appropriate governmental body.

VOLTS: Unit for measuring the force in an electrical current.

WAINSCOTING: A decorative panel, often made of wood, covering the lower part of a wall and sometimes capped by a chair rail.

WORKERS' COMPENSATION INSURANCE: Insurance carried by an employer that protects workers who are injured on the job. Should be carried by all contractors and subcontractors.

ZONING: Government restrictions on the use of a piece of land. Zoning regulations cover such things as what types of structures can be built, how large or small lots and structures can be, and whether the land and structures can be used for residential or commercial purposes. Many houses are located in neighborhoods that are zoned for single-family residences only.

Index

cost-plus, 109–10, 111
   detailed breakdown of, 106
   discussing, with contractors, 111–12
   elements of the job, 107
   extras, 108
   fixed-price, 109, 110
   job reflection, accuracy of, 112
   profit and overhead for contractors, 108
   reimbursable and administrative costs, 107
   signing, appropriate timing for, 112
   supervisor costs, 107
   time-and-materials contract, 111
   underestimating, by contractors, 110
boards of directors, 67, 69
budget
   cost estimates and, 37
   cost-plus arrangements, adverse effects on, 111
   extra living expenses, 44
   for hiring contractors, 95
   for kitchens, 10–11
   limits, communicating, 43
   marriage and, 36
   overextending, 35–36
   planning, 36–37
   rushed remodeler and, 38–39
   splurging, 165, 166
   for unexpected costs, 46–47
building codes, 66
   for additions, 55–56
   for fireplaces, 63
   for roofing materials, 62
building inspectors, 174
building permits
   amending for amended plans, 176
   fees, 127–28
   jobs not requiring, 176
   jobs requiring, 173–74
   obtaining, 98, 127, 128, 173–75
   provisions for, in contracts, 127–28
   records of, keeping, 175
   signing off on, 56, 98, 121, 126, 174
   working without (nonpermitted improvements), 174–75
bullnose tile, 192

cabinetry, 193–94
   installation of, 102, 194
   refacing, 11
   shopping for, 162–63, 166
   types and finishes of, 194
cables, installing, 172
carpentry. See trim and molding
carpeting, 189, 190, 200
caulk, 188

ceiling height, 19
ceiling joists, 184
certificate of occupancy (C of O), 130, 174
change orders, 132, 176
children
   bathrooms for, 16–17
   involving in remodel, 27
   see also safety issues, and children
chimneys, 63, 189
circuit box, 40
circuits, 40
cleanup, 137, 199–200
closets, 20
codes. See building codes
collateral, 49
common areas, 68
comparable sales (comps), 74
completion dates, 128, 129–30, 131
comps (comparable sales), 74
condominiums (condos), 67–69, 181
construction administration phase, 145, 146, 147
construction documents phase, 144, 145, 147
construction loans, 50
construction sites
   neighbors inconvenienced by, 172
   privacy issues, 171–72
   security issues, 170–71
   supplies needed at, 172
contingencies, 107–8, 137
contractors
   being taken advantage by, avoiding, 85–88
   being your own, 82
   bid considerations, when choosing, 104
   building permits obtained by, 127, 128, 175
   company size, considerations when choosing, 87–88
   contacting, 99, 152, 205
   cooperating with, 153
   credentials of, listed on contract, 121
   delays, taking responsibility for, 46, 102
   design/build firms, 88
   desperate, 114, 115
   experience of, 93, 95, 96
   firing, 156–57
   fraud and, 80
   incompetent, signs of, 84–85
   insurance carried by, 98
   landscape, 148
   licensing of, 67, 92, 95
   negotiating with, 115

design development documents, 40
design development phase, 145, 147
design professionals
    hiring, 40–42
    referrals from, 90
    see also interior designers
designs, preliminary, 40
digital photos, 8
dispute resolution, 135–36
downspouts, 187
driveway renovations, 75
drywall, 188

easements, 149
electrical system
    amp capacity, increasing, 58
    circuits and circuit box, 40
    design conveniences, 58
    plans for, 40
    rough work, 185
    safety concerns, 55, 58
    wiring, 18, 58, 172
energy efficiency, 60, 187
engineers
    geologists and soils, 149, 150
    structural, 61, 148–49
entryways, 75
environmental concerns, 187
estimates. *See* cost estimates
expeditors, 150, 176
expenses
    impulse purchases (Might-as-Wells),
        37, 47–48
    of interior designers, 142–43
    living, 44–45
    researching, 43–44
    unexpected (Oh-Nos!), 46–47, 54, 66
extermination, 65, 170

faucets
    pipe pressure and, 59
    safety stops for, 16
    shopping for, 162
field tile, 192
final completion, 130
financing, 48
    cash payments, 49
    construction loans, 50
    contingency, 137
    fees associated with, 49
    home equity loans, 51–52
    loan approval, contract provisions
        for, 50
    payment schedules, listed on
        contract, 123–26
    permanent or take-out loans, 51
    secured real estate loans, 49–50

    see also budget
financing contingency, 137
fireplaces, 63, 166, 189
fixed-price arrangements, 109, 110
fixed-rate loans, 51
fixtures
    bathroom, 162–63, 200
    installation of, 199
    shopping for, 162–63, 166
flipping, 72
flooring
    composite, 191
    concrete, 191
    finished, 184, 189–90
    hardwood, 190–91
    kitchen, 14
    linoleum, 191
    refinished, 75–76
    subflooring, 184
    tile, 191
floor joists, 184
forms, contract, 119
foundations, 61, 183
framing, 184
fumigation, 65
furniture plans, remodeling and, 41

galvanized steel pipes, 59
geologists, 149, 150
governing documents, 67, 68–69
ground fault interrupter (GFI), 58
grout, 193
gutters, 19, 62

hardscaping, 199
hardware, 76, 163
heating, ventilation and air conditioning
    (HVAC)
    asbestos, 63–64
    energy efficiency, 60, 187
    rough work, 185
HGTV, 7
home equity loans, 51–52
home inspections
    for asbestos, 63–64
    of basements, 61
    benefits of, 56–57
    of chimneys, 63
    of foundations, 61
    of gutters, 62
    inspectors, hiring, 57
    for lead, 64–65
    for mold, 64
    for termites, 65
    written reports of, 56
homeowner's associations (HOAs),
    68–69, 127, 169, 182

PITI (principal, interest, taxes, and insurance), 45
planned communities, 67
planning
    details, wish list of, 10
    expectations and, 151–52
    for leadership, 155–56
    organization in, 8
    preparation checklist for, 169–72
    scheduling and, 128
    for unexpected issues, 37, 46–47, 153
    see also plans and specifications (plans and specs)
plans and specifications (plans and specs)
    architects' preparation of, 144
    in contracts, 121–22
    preliminary designs, 40
    questions to ask, 54–56
    size of project and, 40–42, 121
    see also planning
plumbing
    pipes and, 59
    rough, 185
    water pressure and, 59
privacy issues, during remodel, 171–72
progress payments, 123, 124–25
proprietary lease, 68
punch list items, 125, 126, 203–5

references, checking, 98, 100
    from past/current clients, 103–4
    walk-throughs of jobs performed/in progress, 102
    see also referrals
referrals
    from ads, 91
    from architects and designers, 90
    from business and trade organizations, 91
    from real estate brokers, 90
    from relatives, friends, neighbors, 89
    from subcontractors and tradesmen, 90
remodeling
    extent of, 37–38, 57
    extra living expenses, 44
    friends/family and, 30–32
    job and, 32–33
    kids and, 27–28
    new homes, while staying in old, 45–46
    repairs and upgrades, 52–66
    romance and, 26
    rushing, 38–39
    sanity and, preserving, 33

single women and, 28–30
spouse/partners and, 24–27
trends, 74–75
see also trimesters of remodeling
resale value, 71–73
    of best home in the neighborhood, 74–75
    comparable sales (comps) and, 74
    cost-versus-value ratios and, 73
    location and, 73–74
    popular features/trends and, 74
    renovations and, 75–76
research, 6–8
    on costs, 43–44
    Internet and, 6–7
    magazines/TV shows and, 7
    on materials, 11
    organization in, 8
    showrooms/remodels and, 7–8
restrictions, 67
retainage, 125–26
roofs
    building codes for, 62
    fireproofing, 62, 186
    quality of products used for, 187
    tenting and, 62
    types of, 62
    weatherproofing, 186–87

safes, 20
safety issues
    asbestos and, 63–64
    in bathrooms, 16
    electrical wiring and, 55, 58
    fire and, 58, 62, 63, 186
    in home, 55
    lead-based paints and, 64–65
    provisions for, 28
    see also safety issues, and children
safety issues, and children
    in bathrooms, 16
    lead-based paint chips, 65
    during remodel, 27–28
schematic designs, 40
    phase, 145, 147
secured real estate loans, 49–50
security issues, 170–71
shopping
    for appliances, 163
    for bathroom and kitchen fixtures and cabinets, 162–63
    rules of, 164–67
    second opinions and, 167
    for stone, 164
    for tile, 163–64
    unavailable items and, 167
showrooms, 7, 141

About the Authors

Robyn Roth is a Los Angeles native and a graduate of the University of California, Los Angeles, and the Harvard Law School. As a partner for more than a decade in the well-known entertainment law firm currently known as Bloom, Hergott, Diemer, Rosenthal, and LaViolette, LLP, in Beverly Hills, Robyn developed within her extensive law practice a unique specialty: representing individual celebrity and other talent and entertainment industry clients in all of their residential and commercial real estate matters. Unlike most transactional real estate attorneys, whose involvement ends when deals are made and contracts are signed, her job is often only just beginning when the ink is drying. This is because she is a close legal and personal adviser to clients from the time they purchase their properties through the construction, remodeling, and design phases of their projects; she also acts as liaison among her clients and their real estate agents, contractors, architects, designers, and other real estate professionals. She now has her own law firm, continuing to act as real estate attorney, counselor, and confidante to colleagues and clients in the entertainment industry, while at the same time managing her own real estate investments. Robyn brings to the book her personal experience of having purchased and remodeled numerous properties as a single woman.

Laura Meyer is originally from New York City, having graduated from Columbia College and Fordham Law School. After practicing real estate law with one of New York City's top law firms, formerly known Tenzer, Greenblatt, Fallon, and Kaplan, she relocated to Los Angeles to become a divorce/family lawyer and mediator, representing high-profile clientele. Laura not only litigated matrimonial cases but also acted as both a private and court-appointed mediator helping couples to resolve their differences. She counseled her clients through the inevitable real property and other financial quagmires that often emerge in divorces, and witnessed how the stress of remodeling a home can truly be the beginning of the end of a marriage. Laura took a break from the daily practice of law several years ago to devote more time to writing, raising her three young sons, and managing a major home remodel of her own. Laura brings to the book her personal perspective on what it was like to juggle her very trying remodel with her very hectic family life.

Together, Robyn and Laura run **Remodel This!**, a remodeling consultation firm.